101 MEETING STARTERS

➊O➊
MEETING STARTERS

*A Guide to Better
Twelve Step Discussions*

● ● ●

MEL B.

Hazelden
Center City, Minnesota 55012-0176

1-800-328-0094
1-651-213-4590 (Fax)
www.hazelden.org

Library of Congress Cataloging-in-Publication Data
B., Mel.
    101 meeting starters : a guide to better twelve step
    disussions / Mel B.
    p. cm.
    ISBN: 978-1-59285-369-4 (softcover)
    1. Alcoholics—Rehabilitation. 2. Alcoholics Anonymous.
3. Group facilitation. 4. Twelve-step programs. 5. Discussion.
6. Meetings. I. Title. II. Title: One hundred one meeting
starters. III. Title: One hundred and one meeting starters.
HV5275.B2 2007
616.86'106--dc22

                                                    2006046936

11 10 09 08 07   6 5 4 3 2 1

Cover design by David Spohn
Interior design by Ann Sudmeier
Typesetting by Prism Publishing Center

Contents

• • •

❶⓪❶ MEETING STARTERS

Why I Prepared This Guidebook

● ● ●

Discussion meetings are closely tied in with AA's basic purpose of sharing our experience, strength, and hope with each other so we can stay sober and help others achieve sobriety. Certain topics and discussions support this purpose, but others have little or no bearing on sobriety and may even discourage wary newcomers from ever returning to an AA meeting. My hope is that this book will help every AA meeting get started on the right foot, regardless of how skilled the moderator or how distracted the group. My background for writing this book includes steady attendance at AA meetings since 1950. With at least ten thousand meetings behind me, I've come to see that not all AA discussion meetings are equal in content or spirit. Some of them are frightfully boring, although the people attending can be lively and personable. Many meetings go off track quickly, perhaps because they were never firmly on track at the beginning. Moderators sometimes permit discussions to become irrelevant or allow pointless distractions.

One pitfall is to launch meetings around general subjects such as "relationships" or "feelings." These topics are too broad to give us the focus we need for a helpful meeting. I've never come away from such discussions with the belief that we were really dealing with our personal problems. To some people, for example, the word *relationships* has come to mean sexual affairs, while *feelings* could embrace the whole gamut of human emotions.

During one great meeting I recall, a young member admitted to the group that he had been caught shoplifting. We really worked on that topic, and the ensuing discussion allowed some of us to open up about our own past dishonesties. No one condemned the young man, but everybody agreed that shoplifting was wrong and that some amends were necessary. It was a much better meeting than if we had simply tried to discuss the need for honesty.

We also have good meetings when individual members express specific issues that are bothering them at the moment. I recall a woman who was furious because her husband had lost his job, requiring them to move to a town she detested. Resentments of this kind are grist for the AA discussion mill, and almost everybody at the table can bring up examples of similar problems in his or her own past. Discussions can also catch fire when members talk about problems at work or disagreements with co-workers. While some of these discussions may wander a bit, they are healthy because troubled alcoholics need a forum for talking about such matters in a safe environment.

There are times, of course, when certain members will drone on about matters that have little or nothing to do with staying sober. AA even attracts a few people who are badly disturbed or who obsess about certain topics. At such times, it's necessary to get back to the topic at hand, but this should be done with kindness and understanding. I've seen capable moderators break in on such monologues tactfully, changing the subject without hurting feelings.

But our best course is to start the meeting with a good topic or question that will trigger immediate responses in the people at the table. That's why I've written *101 Meeting Starters*. The purpose of this guidebook is to get discussion meetings started in the best way so we will come away fulfilled and happy that we've had another great sharing experience.

Using this guidebook should be simple. The moderator chooses an appropriate topic, or reads a selection of topics aloud to solicit a preference from the group. The moderator then reads the text aloud to start the discussion portion of the meeting. Space has been provided after each topic for taking notes, which can serve as an aid for future discussions.

These topics are not intended to replace good ideas from group members. But they can serve a useful purpose in helping members focus on the problems and concerns that we face in the ongoing quest for continued, happy sobriety.

A Look at Willpower

● ● ●

MODERATOR: In AA, we don't believe that will-power can keep us sober. Most of us tried that route before we got here, and it didn't work for us. No matter how much we "willed" ourselves to get sober and stay that way, we always wound up drunk. This was a frustrating business, and some of us decided we were just too weak-willed to find sobriety.

But many alcoholics are very strong-willed, and this can even be part of the problem. The will is our power to make choices and carry through with them. In drinking, however, we've acquired a compulsion that makes the wrong choices. The more we fight this compulsion, the more it tightens its grip on us. (People with other compulsions understand this well, hence the saying that "you can't eat just one potato chip.")

The process that seems to work for us in AA is to choose a different path with the understanding that our Higher Power is working in and through us, as well as over and above us. Our own will then becomes only the power to choose, but it is not the power that does the actual work of keeping us sober.

For this to work, we have to believe in the process and accept it for ourselves. It is simple, but it works. Now I'd like to ask the group to recall efforts to stay sober on willpower alone. Most likely, these efforts worked for a time and then failed. I need a volunteer to start the discussion with an example from personal experience.

....

....

....

....

....

....

....

....

....

....

....

....

....

....

....

....

....

Am I Different?

● ● ●

MODERATOR: Most of us think we are different, and in some ways we are. As alcoholics, we had similar problems, but we each had our own drinking patterns and other unique traits. One of our biggest jobs, then, is to convince people that they might be alcoholics just like the rest of us.

One delusion that has to be crushed is the belief that we might someday find the ability to do controlled drinking. Some people say it can be done, but they aren't in AA, and they probably don't have proof that it works. Some alcoholics are also brighter and more successful than the rest of us. But we have enough bright, successful people in AA to show that these advantages are of little help in overcoming alcoholism. Alcoholism appears to be an equal-opportunity disease that targets people at every level in society. It's also a delusion to believe that we don't have a problem simply because other people had more trouble with alcohol than we seem to have. We don't have to go through everything that some other person endured in order to admit that we're powerless over alcohol. Just as with any other ailment, we can be grateful that we're dealing with it in the earlier stages.

So we are the same in having the problem, though we are different in some respects. Who will start the discussion by explaining how "being different" was a problem that had to be dealt with in getting sober?

Are Alcoholics Perfectionists?

● ● ●

MODERATOR: Now and then we'll hear AA speakers say that they used to be perfectionists. This seems a strange thing to hear from people who, when drinking, most likely turned in sloppy work as employees or halfheartedly approached life's responsibilities. We might think that trying to be perfect, or doing tasks perfectly, is a good thing. Then why is it a personal problem?

One answer may be that even though we strive to be perfect, we live in a reality that is far from perfect. Perfectionists might be hoping for achievements and conditions that are far beyond anything that is possible here and now. Part of our problem with life is that nothing measures up to the pictures we carry in our heads. That's how perfectionism can cause us trouble.

In our effort to make perfectionism less of a problem, we need to find satisfaction in small but frequent improvements rather than in the smashing successes of our dreams. If we can't make home runs all the time, we have to know that games are often won with single-base hits. And most of the people around us don't have the luxury of being perfectionists. They have to be satisfied with progress rather than perfection.

Bill W. said that the good can be the enemy

of the best. But there's also a saying in engineering that good enough is best. If what we're doing today is good enough, it may be as perfect as it needs to be.

In any case, we have to quit living in perfectionistic dreams and start accepting the reality around us. Who has some thoughts to share on this topic?

....

....

....

....

....

....

....

....

....

....

....

....

....

....

Are We Passing It On?

● ● ●

MODERATOR: When people met Bill W. for the first time and expressed their gratitude to him, his usual answer was "Pass it on." This became the title of his biography, published by AA World Services. It has also become a slogan in AA.

Unfortunately, people can pass on bad ideas as well as good ones. A number of recovering alcoholics feel real guilt over the bad things they passed on while they were drinking. Some are sicker than others, of course, and some have done terrible things while others have injured only themselves for the most part. But the truth is that very little good is passed on while we drink.

In AA, we have the opportunity to pass on principles and actions that can be of real benefit to others, including people we will never meet. If we create active groups that really carry the message, we will be passing on things that will endure long after we're no longer in the picture. If our AA experience enables us to take responsibility for our family's well-being, our family members will benefit and so will society as a whole. When we "pass it on," we are also paying any debt we might have to the people who carried the message to us.

How do we pass it on in AA terms? One of the best ways is to keep the group functioning as a place where newcomers can find hope and recovery. This means that future newcomers—people whom Bill W. called "the million who still don't know"— can find the same recovery that was presented to us.

Perhaps we can now have a volunteer who will give a personal view of passing it on.

Are We Victims?

●●●

MODERATOR: Today's topic is a question: Are we victims? Undoubtedly, we've been called victims of alcoholism and may have even used such terms ourselves as a way of not taking personal responsibility for our drinking. Most of us don't have much confidence when we get here. Maybe we believe we can preserve a shred of self-esteem by saying we were victimized by something beyond our control.

But as we look over the entire program, we can see that there's not much room for victimhood here. All along the way, most of us thought we were calling the shots. We probably had plenty of warnings, but we plunged ahead with the certain feeling that we weren't like those other drunks who had fallen by the wayside. It wouldn't happen to us. Then, when it did happen to us, we probably tried to deny it. And of course, it's necessary to cut through this denial phase in order to accept the AA program.

Once we're into the program, nobody gives us much slack. We are urged to take a personal inventory, clear up the wreckage of the past, find a Higher Power, and do something to help others. Not much talk of being a victim here.

It is true that we have succumbed to a condition that we choose to call a disease. Other people are more hard-nosed about this and simply say that we did it to ourselves. It doesn't make much difference which view we accept as long as we understand that we are alcoholics and cannot safely take even one drink.

If we were victims, we were really victimized only by our own bad thinking and wrong actions. Now we can be survivors and leave the victimhood to others.

Is there a former victim who would like to start the discussion?

....

....

....

....

....

....

....

....

....

....

....

....

Attracting Trouble

● ● ●

MODERATOR: While many of us got lucky breaks even while drinking, there were also times when everything worked against us. We were driving drunk just when tough cops showed up, we wound up with bosses who seemed unfair, we had friends who betrayed us. What's surprising is that some of us have the same kind of bad luck in sobriety. We don't get DUIs anymore, but we still have trouble with people or get into work and business situations that turn into disasters. We may have marriage and relationship problems that have nothing to do with drinking.

Part of this trouble can be chalked up to the human condition. The price of being human is that we have to be involved in the struggles and disputes that go on almost everywhere. Being AA members doesn't automatically give us immunity from the problems common in society.

But there are times when we seem to attract more than our share of troubles. When such things happen, it's time to take inventory to see what we're doing that might be attracting such misfortune into our lives. Maybe we're looking for approval from the wrong people. Maybe we're doing something that violates our principles. Maybe we've been expecting too much from people and situations that really can't give us what we want or need.

Who can give an example of dealing with a personal tendency to attract trouble?

....

....

....

....

....

....

....

....

....

....

....

....

....

....

Be Careful What You Pray For

● ● ●

MODERATOR: In choosing the topic for today, I'm assuming that everybody here has some experience with AA and that there's a general agreement that prayer and meditation help us to stay sober.

We're sometimes warned that we should be careful what we pray for. Another form of this warning is "Be careful what you wish for." Prayers and wishes are currents of thought directed toward specific goals. If we focus our thinking on something for a period of time, it is likely to appear in our lives. This is an exciting idea, one that's been around for a long time. We can control our thinking even if there are lots of other things in the world that seem to be beyond our control. We can decide what we're going to think about, and we can choose to turn our thinking in certain directions.

The warning is that we should pray only about outcomes that we want to see in our lives. We should be particularly careful not to focus on things that can be harmful for us or others. We shouldn't want things that are beyond our capacity to handle. The Eleventh Step gives us a good blueprint for prayer. We should pray only for knowledge of God's will for us and the power to carry that out. Even there, however, we have to think carefully about what we're doing. How can we know what God's will for us is? Have we had any proof that this works? Those are questions we ought to discuss. Who will be the first to offer an opinion?

Being Responsible

● ● ●

MODERATOR: I'd like to suggest the subject of being responsible as a meeting topic today. What does being responsible mean for the recovering alcoholic? What and whom are we responsible for? When do we know that we're really being responsible for our decisions and actions? One thing we do know is that, for the alcoholic, responsibility and drinking don't go together. We may want to be responsible, but drinking makes that impossible. More than likely, many of us slipped to the point where others had to take responsibility for some of the damage we did.

Bill W. wrote about the way alcoholics seek protectors—people who can help us get out of financial and legal troubles. In time, protectors either get out of our space or are no longer able to help us. After all, who wants to be responsible for people who won't do anything to help themselves? AA's experience even tells us that *we* shouldn't stay involved with people who don't want to quit drinking; otherwise, we become enablers—we start to take responsibility for their problems too.

Being responsible for ourselves becomes possible when we get sober. It may be painful at times, and it may require dropping some old attitudes that weren't very good anyway. But if we take responsibility in various kinds of situations, we'll also discover ourselves growing into the kind of maturity that alcoholics usually need. We sometimes hear that we need higher self-esteem. But there's nothing like taking responsibility to help us grow in self-esteem.

What kinds of responsibility are we talking about? For starters, how about being financially responsible and facing our debts and shortcomings? Who will offer a personal experience that will help start the discussion?

Changing Things We Can

● ● ●

MODERATOR: The Serenity Prayer tells us that we ought to change the things we can while accepting the things we can't. We should also find the wisdom to know the difference between the two.

The Serenity Prayer implies that we should only try to change things that concern us; we certainly can't be expected to change things over which we have no control. But in order to change the things we can change, we have to show a certain amount of courage, which may be in short supply if we have been hiding our problems by drinking.

We put up with things in our lives that could be changed for many reasons. We may fear facing something that could be unpleasant, for example. Sometimes it seems easier to stay in the old behavior, or the old rut, than it does to make a change that would be better for everybody concerned. Suppose, for example, that we've been having problems with someone at work or in another setting. Changing this situation may require sitting down with the person and laying it all out. That takes courage, but it can also put an end to an unbearable situation.

Some AA members have regretted not having more schooling or training. But with enough courage, it's possible for a person to go back and hit the books at any age. A surprising number of AA members have done that, and it has helped to change their lives. Making necessary amends always requires a bit of courage, but it always pays off when we do it. A great example of this is Dr. Bob's story in the Big Book.

At this time, let's look at things we've been putting off out of fear, such as a medical exam. Who has other examples to start the discussion?

Coming to Grips with Fear

● ● ●

MODERATOR: Many of us did not like to admit it while we were still drinking, but we can now see that fear played a big part in our alcoholism. There were times when we dove into the bottle because we were afraid, and this only had the effect of creating more situations that caused more fear. We've all had such experiences. We feared being confronted by bill collectors, for example, and then got drunk and created more debt. We feared getting fired, and by getting drunk we made it happen.

Fear doesn't go away just because we're no longer drinking. So the topic for this meeting is "coming to grips with fear." In sobriety, how can we cope with fear in ways that make it work *for* us rather than *against* us?

When fear comes up as a topic, someone is likely to point out that fear is necessary to help get us out of the way of an oncoming truck. But we're talking here about the kind of fear that freezes us in our tracks when we see a truck coming.

The truck, of course, is any threat or big problem in our lives. We have all kinds of them in different forms, and if we're going to be sober and happy, we have to deal with them. Here are just a few examples of irrational fears that hinder us:

1. Being afraid to go to the doctor when symptoms appear, even though early detection of any ailment is always critical in the treatment.
2. Being afraid to make a move in one's own best interest, such as applying for a job or asking somebody for a date.
3. Being afraid to open letters from creditors or to take any steps to get one's financial affairs in order.

These are only a few examples, but we can certainly find others. Who will begin by sharing an example of coming to grips with fear while also living sober?

....

....

....

....

....

....

....

....

Contending with Self-Will

● ● ●

MODERATOR: According to the Big Book, self-will is one of our major problems as alcoholics. In the chapter titled "How It Works," we read that our troubles are basically of our own making. "They arise out of ourselves," it says, "and the alcoholic is an extreme example of self-will run riot, though he usually doesn't think so." And the book warns, "Above everything, we alcoholics must be rid of this selfishness. We must, or it kills us!"

This is quite a statement, and some of us may have trouble fitting ourselves into this category. We may have thought we were the victims of other people's selfishness, not our own. So it may take some time and a great deal of soul-searching to understand and accept this.

What's even more confusing is that some people call AA a selfish program, but they mean it in a good way: It's something you accept in order to save yourself. So if selfishness is good in this sense, why is it bad otherwise? That's why this is a good topic for discussion. Everybody has to practice a certain amount of self-protection in order to survive, but when does it become a problem? Why was self-ishness so destructive while we were drinking?

The problem must be rooted in the emotions that were driving us. Most of the time, alcoholics are feeding unhealthy needs in destructive ways. In recovery, we still have needs, but they can be met in better ways. A sick alcoholic, for example, may meet his need for self-esteem by buying drinks for everybody in the bar, at his family's expense. A recovering person finds self-esteem by living in the right way and by meeting responsibilities. Even in sobriety, however, the old demon of selfishness will raise its ugly head. Who has some experience to share on this topic?

Controlling the Imagination

● ● ●

MODERATOR: One of the things that works for us in AA is to use our imagination to see ourselves living sober lives. We get that idea in the Big Book chapter titled "A Vision for You." We should put our imagination to work and let it weave some pictures of ourselves reaping and enjoying the fruits of sober living. Used in this way, our imagination can be a powerful force for good in our lives. We should also remember that our imagination has worked against us in the past. Each of us has had many times when we wanted to stay sober and then started imagining what was going on in our favorite tavern. Before we knew it, we were headed for the bar even though we knew it was the wrong thing to do.

There is an old saying to the effect that when our will and our imagination are in conflict, our imagination always wins. That being so, we should take care to focus our imagination only on the things we want to have in our lives.

With a little effort and discipline, we can build pictures of ourselves living in the circumstances that can be created when we stay sober. We can see ourselves living responsibly, getting rid of guilt from the past, and going through the day completely free of alcohol or the need to take a drink.

It helps to see other AA members as role models who are living good lives in sobriety. If drinking has impoverished us, we can picture ourselves enjoying at least a modest level of prosperity and earning our own living. We can picture lots of other benefits as we begin to trudge what the Big Book calls the "road of happy destiny."

Like most of our other gifts, the human imagination can be a good servant even after it has been a terrible master. Who has experience along this line to share?

....

....

....

....

....

....

....

....

....

....

....

....

Coping with Depression

● ● ●

MODERATOR: Mention the problem of depression at an AA meeting, and you're likely to see quite a few people nodding in agreement. Even in sobriety, depression can hit many of us, and it's neither pleasant nor constructive when it happens.

How do we cope with depression? Well, the very first thing to keep in mind is that we won't drink, no matter how depressed we are. With most of us, our moods can swing from depression to mild elation, and we have to stay in charge no matter which mood we're in.

Some people in AA take medications for depression, while others frown on the practice and think it may lead to drinking. That's something to discuss with your doctor, because we're not supposed to practice medicine one way or another unless we really are doctors.

We know that Bill W. suffered from profound depression and had to find his own methods of dealing with it. He discovered that taking walks seemed to help him, although he had to discipline himself to do it. Bill also looked upon depression as a problem that seems to heal itself over time.

We must have a few people at this meeting who have gone through some depressed times. Can we have a volunteer who will share personal experience on this subject?

Coping with Social Pressure

● ● ●

MODERATOR: We don't talk about it often in AA, but there is a thing called "social pressure" that alcoholics have to cope with in recovery. Social pressure comes in several forms and hits people at all ages and all levels of society. With young people, we often call it "peer pressure," but it's the same whether you're thirteen or thirty-five or seventy.

In North America, we live in a sea of alcohol. As we navigate our way in this sea, our situation is like that of a real ship at sea. And the rule for a real ship is that all the water in the ocean cannot sink the ship unless the water gets inside. The same is true for alcoholics. All the booze around us cannot defeat us unless it gets inside—unless we take a drink.

Taking that a step further, we can also say that we will never take a drink unless our thinking causes us to. We can be surrounded by active drinkers, but we don't have to join them in drinking. Few people would be so mean-spirited as to pressure an alcoholic to drink when they know it means disaster. But they can unknowingly create pressure with their comments and attitudes. A friend might say, "You've been sober two years. Surely you ought to be able to drink now." Another person might ask, "How long are you going to stay on the wagon?" And there are a few people who will raise their eyebrows when they learn you're having a soft drink instead of an alcoholic beverage at a party. Special occasions, such as weddings and anniversaries, are also seen as reasons to drink excessively, even for people who rarely take a drink.

How are we to handle ourselves in these situations? Whatever we do, our primary need is to stay sober under any and all conditions. So let's throw the subject out on the table to see how the group feels about social pressure, sometimes called peer pressure.

Dealing with Disagreeable People

● ● ●

MODERATOR: One of the topics that comes up regularly in AA is the problem of dealing with disagreeable people, whether they be spouses, ex-spouses, parents, siblings, neighbors, bosses, customers, or co-workers. Whatever the relationship, we find ourselves reacting to them in unpleasant ways, leaving us with fear, resentment, bitterness, disgust, or anxiety. We keep trying out new ways to deal with them, and nothing seems to work.

How can we deal with disagreeable people effectively while protecting our sobriety and our mental well-being? The Twelve Step program gives us some useful approaches. The first thing to remember is that the problem is with us, not the other person. This is spelled out in the "Twelve and Twelve"—that is, the book *Twelve Steps and Twelve Traditions*—where it says that whenever we're disturbed, we're at fault. This means that we set ourselves up. People press our buttons, but we put the buttons there for them to press.

We can get these people out of our lives by moving, getting a divorce, or quitting our job, but the surprising thing is that we might meet the same kinds of people in any new situation. We don't solve problems by running away from them.

The program's answer is to put on our spiritual

armor. We turn all of these people and problems over to our Higher Power, recognizing that they have rights too and are children of God just as we are. We should also search for anything we might be doing that feeds the problem. We might be expecting too much of others and of ourselves. But as we change our own thinking, our relationships must also change. Who will give us examples of this from his or her life?

....

....

....

....

....

....

....

....

....

....

....

Dealing with Rejection

● ● ●

MODERATOR: Rejection doesn't seem to come up often as a meeting topic, but it certainly ought to be discussed in AA. I haven't read any studies on it, but it's fair to say that alcoholics as a group don't take kindly to rejection. Most of us are thin-skinned, and rejection of any kind can hurt. It can leave us feeling unworthy and less acceptable than others.

This type of thinking is unrealistic and shows that we need more understanding about how the world works. Rejection is a fact of life. We can't avoid being rejected now and then, and we also can't avoid rejecting others in various ways.

One of the most hurtful kinds of rejection is being turned down for employment, especially when we're badly in need of work. The reality is that a number of applicants apply for one job opening, which means that most people will have to be rejected when the opening is filled. We should not take such a rejection personally—but sometimes we do, and this causes problems for us.

It's also common to get rejected in love. Some of us carry resentments about this sort of rejection for a long time. When we do, we're being very foolish, because such rejections are usually for our own good—although we don't see it that way when we're being turned down. Some lines of work also involve getting rejected on an ongoing basis. In most sales jobs, for example, the salesperson is lucky if more than a small percentage of her contacts results in a sale. If she took each turndown personally, she would become a nervous wreck. Because rejection is a fact of life, perhaps the topic today should be "How does the AA program help us deal with rejection in a mature way?"

Dealing with the Past

● ● ●

MODERATOR: In AA, we're supposed to let go of the wreckage of the past and go on with our lives in sobriety. This is good advice, but some of us have a hard time following it. The past has a way of coming back to haunt us and even hurt us.

The biggest damage is the harm we do to ourselves by brooding about the past and wishing that things could have been different. But of course nothing could have been different, because we thought and acted in ways that either brought trouble directly or put us in positions to be hurt.

There's a more sinister side to this, and that's in wishing harm to those who hurt us. We see this often in AA when an aggrieved person will talk angrily about a former spouse who seemed to be the problem. The harm was so great, the troubled person believes, that it cannot or should not be forgiven. Quite often, the harm ends the day of the divorce, and yet the person holds on to those grievances. This is very close to insanity, and it causes continuing damage.

Here is another way the past haunts us: somebody may criticize us in a mild way, and we explode with anger. The criticism has triggered bad memories of times when we were criticized almost unmercifully.

We have to get past all of these things in sober living. And now is the time to do it. If we're going to be happy and successful in the here and now, we can't bring along the garbage of the past. This might be a good topic for discussion today. How about some thoughts from a person who had a problem with the past and found a way to deal with it?

Do Material Things Matter?

● ● ●

MODERATOR: The topic for today is about dealing with the material conditions in our lives. Most AA members had money problems while drinking, and some of us continue to be plagued by debt and unemployment. Is there anything in the AA program that helps us to face these problems?

We have a good example in the story of the founding of AA. When Bill W. and Dr. Bob met for the first time, both were reeling from money problems. Bill, though sober, had just undergone a bad setback in business. Dr. Bob, still drinking, had lost some of his medical practice and even feared that he would be ousted from the profession. Yet both of them survived and lived with a fair amount of comfort for the rest of their lives.

As far as we know, neither of them denounced the making of money or took vows of poverty. Most of the alcoholics they worked with in the beginning were also broke and had to deal with money problems. How did they work them out?

They focused first on the need to get sober and stay that way. Practicing the principle of "First things first," they dealt with the drinking problems, which were also a cause of their money troubles. But along the way, we can be sure that they realized that money problems can also hit people who are staying sober and doing the best they can to live rightly.

The AA program is no guarantee that we won't have the money problems that most people have to face. However, it *is* a guarantee that if we stay sober, we won't be making our money problems worse by the weird things we do while drinking.

It would be interesting to know what steps those of us here have taken to deal responsibly with money. Can we have a volunteer to get the discussion going?

....

....

....

....

....

....

....

....

....

....

Do We Deserve Success?

• • •

MODERATOR: The topic I'd like us to consider to-day is "Do we deserve success?" I'm not just talking about success in making money and winning recognition. We should consider the matter of succeeding in all walks of life.

There is a belief that alcoholics are the kind of people who snatch defeat from the jaws of victory. We hear stories all the time about people who build up successful businesses or reach a respectable position and then do something stupid that brings the whole thing crashing down. It's sometimes called "shooting yourself in the foot," and we do it all the time.

This can go on in sobriety as well as in drinking. Putting the plug in the jug can eliminate some of the worst problems, but we'll find others even in our new way of life. And we can be sure that many AA members have asked such questions as "Why am I my own worst enemy?" or "Why did I do such a stupid thing?"

We can only speculate about the reasons for some of our self-defeating behaviors. But if we truly live the program, we should start feeling that we deserve success. We may encounter the usual blows that come to people everywhere, but we should be able to take these in stride and go on with whatever we're doing. In any case, we should not let guilt over our past lives hamper our progress today. If we have admitted our wrongs, made amends, and turned matters over to our Higher Power, we should expect the successes that others enjoy. Is there someone in the group who has had to cope with this problem and found answers in the program?

Does AA Meet Wants or Needs?

●●●

MODERATOR: An important question to ask our-selves is "What do we have that other people should want?" We feel that they should want sobriety as a basic need if they are truly alcoholic. Unfortunately, many of us also have a list of unmet wants as well as unmet needs, and we get them confused.

Wants and needs are not always the same, al-though they can be. When we were drinking, we may have wanted a lot of things that turned out to be destructive. In sobriety, we can't want destructive things if we hope to survive and live peacefully in society. We also know that merely getting what we want does not necessarily lead to sober living. We've seen many alcoholics who, after getting back their jobs or getting their creditors off their backs or per-haps getting a break from a lenient judge, think they can drink again.

Even being in AA cannot guarantee that all our wants will be met on demand, even the positive things. A number of people who come to AA don't like to hear that the main goal we work for is sobri-ety, and even those who want it don't like to hear that sobriety is something people must seek for themselves.

We can say, however, that most sober people can move on to face the other wants and needs in their lives. There is no guarantee that this will happen in every case, but common sense tells us that a sober person can function better in society than a person who is drunk or hungover much of the time. You might not get a new car right away, but at least you won't get any more DUIs while driving the old one.

We must have a number of people here who had to change their focus in order to get sober and stay that way. May we have a volunteer to start discussion of this subject?

Does Alcoholism Have a Physical Origin?

● ● ●

MODERATOR: From its very beginning, AA accepted the belief that alcoholism is partly the result of an "allergy." Even though this belief was put in writing for the Big Book by a doctor, it has been a tough sell with the medical profession. After all, most allergies produce an unpleasant reaction rather than the surge of excitement alcoholics get from drinking. Perhaps it would be better to say that alcoholics have a physical susceptibility to alcohol. Nobody can really say whether this susceptibility is inborn or acquired. But it's almost certain that alcoholics seem to get an unusual buzz from drinking that other drinkers don't experience. In fact, it would be difficult for most moderate drinkers to drink excessively.

How does this information help us in recovery? For one thing, it's good to know the facts about our problem. We must face the hard truth that we are indeed different from social drinkers and cannot safely take even one drink without sliding into disaster. It's also useful to know that this physical susceptibility is only one part of our alcoholism. Another component of our addiction is emotional immaturity, bad thinking, and grandiose feelings and behaviors—believing or acting as if we are better or more important than others. All of these can be dealt with by following the principles outlined in the Twelve Steps.

Maybe a useful topic for discussion is what those of us here think about the roots of our alcoholism. Would somebody like to share personal feelings about this subject?

....

....

....

....

....

....

....

....

....

....

....

....

....

Does "Easy Does It" Do It?

● ● ●

MODERATOR: "Easy does it" is one of the three slogans given in the AA Big Book. It suggests living in a way that reduces the anxiety and pressure that happen in everyday life. The basic idea behind this slogan is that there is a calmer, simpler approach to life and work that is much better than the way we conducted ourselves in the past. Does it work? We have to find that out for ourselves as we continue to follow the program. Here are some practices that might be automatically eliminated when we apply "Easy does it" to everyday living:

1. Being pushy to gain an advantage, such as speeding in heavy traffic.
2. Trying to win useless arguments by talking over other people and cutting in on another person. For a good example of a bad example, look at the way people sometimes argue on television programs featuring so-called experts.
3. Working too hard at times and loafing too much at other times. Either is an extreme that should be avoided.
4. Being too hard on ourselves or on others. Taking a relaxed approach actually gives us the energy and calm confidence we need to

do things more effectively. We will still reach our goals but without the wear and tear that pushing and pounding creates in so many lives.

Who can give us a good example of practicing "Easy does it"?

....

....

....

....

....

....

....

....

....

....

....

....

....

Does Harm Reduction Work?

● ● ●

MODERATOR: The concept of harm reduction might not be familiar to everybody here, but it has been around for a while as one approach to dealing with alcoholism. Harm reduction is when an alcoholic makes efforts to reduce the quantity and frequency of his or her drinking. It also involves encouraging the alcoholic to avoid actions that might result in harm to the alcoholic or others. For example, alcoholics might be trained to turn their car keys over to friends before taking a drink.

We shouldn't criticize any effort to help alcoholics, even though our belief is that, to recover, the alcoholic must stay abstinent. And it's true that some alcoholics do structure their lives in such a way that they can minimize short-term damage while they drink.

But it's also likely that most of the people at this meeting tried to devise their own harm-reduction methods while they were still drinking. There might have been some brief successes followed by even more trouble. In any case, we all wound up in AA, where we hope to avoid harm completely rather than just reduce it.

Perhaps we could share some of those stories today. They might be helpful to members who are still harboring the idea that their drinking wasn't all that bad and that maybe they could start drinking again without having all the pain and trouble that made them seek out AA.

Would anyone like to begin?

Emotional Sobriety

• • •

MODERATOR: After Bill W. died in 1971, we learned that he had suffered from deep depression and had other shortcomings. But Bill had always reminded us that he had trouble living up to all the ideals of the program, and he also explained that he had not found what he called "emotional sobriety." It's reasonable to say that he was talking about the problems we associate with being in a "dry drunk." In a dry drunk, we are not drinking, but our feelings are way out of control. This happens when we suffer from depression, fear, anger, resentment, jealousy, and all the other emotions that, when out of proportion, can get human beings into so much trouble. The further complication for AA members is that when our emotions are out of whack, we feel guilty about it. And there seems to be two types of emotional binges. One type has a specific cause, while the other type comes and goes without rhyme or reason.

Here's an emotional binge with a specific cause: the creditors are hounding you, the bank is about to foreclose on your house, and then you're told that your job is being terminated about the same time your spouse has taken up with someone else. Who wouldn't be upset? In such a case, the goal is to get through the upheaval without taking a drink, even when everything seems to be falling apart.

The other kind of emotional binge may be more common for recovering people. Even when things are going well, our emotions just don't behave. For no apparent reason, we can be depressed, unreasonably elated, or unreasonably angry. Panic attacks hit many of us. Here again, the job is to get through these episodes without taking a drink.

We can talk about these problems and how we deal with them. Who will begin by recalling a time of emotional distress and your personal effort to survive it?

Erasing the Old Tapes

● ● ●

MODERATOR: Technology has given us terms for some of the problems that have always plagued the human race. Some terms are becoming outdated in our digital age, but they still work. When you hear an AA member talk about "playing the old tapes," for example, you know that person is referring to re-hashing old grievances and complaints so that they still create trouble today.

These are memories and problems that cannot help us today, and yet we hang on to them. The only value in these "old tapes" is in showing us where we still need work. We should ask ourselves why we're still playing the old tapes and what we can do to erase them.

Two kinds of old tapes can give us trouble. One kind remembers all the hurts, grievances, disappointments, and failures of the past. The more we hang on to these and continue to replay them, the more trouble we'll have in finding happiness in sobriety.

The second kind of old tape might be even more deadly. This one recalls drinking experiences and so-called good times that involved alcohol. We can't afford to indulge this kind of thinking for any longer than it takes us to reject it. If we still think drinking can bring us something good, we're still on the edge of trouble. And we should never let these old tapes lure us into drinking situations.

Does anybody here have something to share on this topic? Who has had trouble with—or has learned how to erase—the old tapes?

Fearing Change

• • •

MODERATOR: We sometimes hear that alcoholics don't like change. This is odd because our drinking usually brought lots of changes, mostly unpleasant ones. And whether we liked it or not, we had changes thrust upon us.

The reality of life is that change is going on all the time. Our challenge is not to fight change but to work within it so that it brings positive outcomes rather than loss and hurt. And sometimes even the unpleasant changes can have surprisingly beneficial outcomes.

Some alcoholics have even been able to transform the unpleasant changes of the past into advantages. Mike E., the second AA member to get sober in Detroit, had been fired from an executive position in a rather humiliating way. He found sobriety, forgave the man who had humiliated him, and went on to operate a small shop that grew into a manufacturing company employing hundreds of people. Other AA members, however, have intentionally made changes that didn't work out as planned, but they learned important lessons.

Changes are also brought about by illness, failed marriages, economic recession, and accidents. As much as possible, we try to deal constructively with such crises by recalling and following our principles. But whether we see changes as good or bad, they are occurring all the time, and we cannot prevent them even if we want to.

If we look at human progress in total, we must admit that change has given us the advancement we seek and desire. Change is good for humankind, but how do we deal with the change we fear as individuals? Who will offer an example from personal experience?

Finding a Higher Power

● ● ●

MODERATOR: One of the surprising chapters in the AA Big Book is the one titled "We Agnostics." Many of us liked to say that we were agnostics, and we even felt that this made us open-minded and fair. Some of us may have even felt that our agnosticism made us superior to the religious people whom we considered narrow-minded and hypocritical.

Then AA gave us a jolt by suggesting that we needed a Higher Power in order to find and maintain sobriety. At every meeting, we're told that no human power can relieve our alcoholism, but God can and will if he is sought.

There are many reasons why we can believe that a Higher Power exists in the universe. It is certain that an amazing intelligence can be seen everywhere in nature and in the universe itself. There is also a creative process at work in the way the earth appeared and in how life has evolved over millions of years. But none of that means much to us until we find a Higher Power in our own lives.

The Big Book tells us that we find our Higher Power by turning our lives over to God as we understand God and then continuing to seek God through prayer and meditation. If we discover that this leads to continued sobriety and changes our lives for the better, we have discovered something very important.

This experience will count for more in our lives than any theories that prove or cast doubt on the existence of God. If our new beliefs work constructively in our own lives, we have achieved success in finding a God of our understanding.

Who will share a personal experience in finding a Higher Power?

Finding God's Will for Us

● ● ●

MODERATOR: I've chosen a tough topic today, but the AA program calls for a discussion of it. The Eleventh Step says that we ought to pray and meditate in seeking God's will for us and the power to carry that out. The trouble with this is that we might not really know whether we are seeking God's will or just following our own inclinations, which might not be all that good for us or others. So is there any way we can determine what God's will is for us as individuals? The AA pioneers believed that this part of the program was essential in getting sober and staying that way. Our purpose here is very serious, and we want to follow principles that will aid us in our own recovery and the recovery of others.

We can test ourselves and others when we question whether we are receiving God's guidance by considering the following points: whatever we plan to do, or feel that we've been guided to do, should be fair and honest, with harm to nobody. It should measure up to good moral principles. It should be reasonable, and if it seems unreasonable, we should discuss it with someone whose judgment we trust. Bill W., for example, had a sudden spiritual illumination that defied reason. He checked it with his doctor, who told him to hang on to it, saying, "Anything's better than the way you were."

As I said, this is a tough topic, so I'll pass it on to the group here. Who will be the first to offer some thoughts?

Finding True Independence

• • •

MODERATOR: The goal of personal freedom is very important to alcoholics. Yet we indulge in behavior that is almost guaranteed to make us slavishly dependent on others. These unhealthy relationships have been called codependent relationships. How do we get out of these situations after we've achieved continuous sobriety?

We can begin by taking a personal inventory that shows us how and why we've been dependent. Quite likely, we'll even find that we've been dependent on people we secretly resented or even hated. They might be people who seemed square and stodgy while we were daring and liberated. But when we got into trouble, we turned to the square and stodgy people for help.

Finding true independence also requires us to grow up and accept responsibilities that we've been avoiding. This can be a painful process for a person who has been escaping into the bottle for years.

We'll also have to learn what true independence really is. It is not being completely divorced from the need for other people in our lives. We should even be able to see that some kinds of dependency are reasonable and normal.

Bill W. used the example of dependency on electricity as something that actually gives us more freedom. We can also depend on people to provide things that we cannot provide for ourselves. But this should be carried out in the right way, which we'll understand as we continue to live sober and grow in right thinking.

Who can start by offering an example of growth into true independence?

....

....

....

....

....

....

....

....

....

....

....

....

....

....

First Things First: Getting Things in Order

● ● ●

MODERATOR: We have some great slogans in our program. But how do we use them in our lives? And why are they important for those of us in recovery?

One of these slogans, right out of the Big Book, is "First things first." Bill W. often used the example of "trying to put the cart before the horse." A horse can pull a cart, but it's not very good at pushing one. So you have to put the horse first if you want to get anything done.

It's the same way with living sober. We have to put certain actions first in order to get the results we're expecting. We might not be good organizers, but we can make an effort to get somewhat organized.

The very first order of business, for any alcoholic, is to stay sober today. That has to come first. For many of us, that means getting in touch with our Higher Power when we start the day. The next thing might be something as basic as getting to work on time. And after that, it could be something such as taking the time to repair a broken relationship, or at least thinking rightly about it.

One of our friends had his priorities set up this way: sobriety came first, then his job, and then his family. He reasoned that if he took care of sobriety, he could do his job, which then meant that he could support his family. It worked for him.

As a topic today, I'd like to ask the group to share examples of using the slogan "First things first" to good advantage. Who will start the discussion?

....

....

....

....

....

....

....

....

....

....

....

....

....

....

....

Getting Beyond People Pleasing

● ● ●

MODERATOR: One of the odd things we hear alcoholics say at meetings is that they were people pleasers. This is odd because almost nobody is pleased with an alcoholic's behavior. Why do we say that we were people pleasers when we pleased so few people and angered so many?

One explanation for this may be the low self-esteem so many of us had and still have to some degree. A lawyer in AA said that she had always charged her clients less than other lawyers would have billed for the same services. She was feeling inadequate as a lawyer, perhaps because of her excessive drinking, so she was making up for it by giving her clients bargain rates. She was saying, in effect, "I want to please you so you'll come back to me instead of finding a first-rate lawyer."

There can also be the guilt and remorse we feel as alcoholics. Having neglected normal responsibilities, we may go overboard by doing more than our share at other times. This never really works, but we can delude ourselves into thinking that it does. Finally, we can be tyrannized by that nagging desire to be liked. If we break our necks to please somebody, maybe that person will like us. What we're saying is, "You owe me your approval and friendship because of everything I'm doing to please you.

Sure, I'm a drunk, but look at all the other nice things I do."

Well, it's nice to have friends and to be liked, but reality tells us that, regardless of what we do, not everybody will like us. We must not let ourselves be either used or abused, and if we understand that properly, we can learn how to relate to people in acceptable ways.

Who here has had a problem being a people pleaser, and how did you get beyond it?

....

....

....

....

....

....

....

....

....

....

....

....

Giving Away to Keep

● ● ●

MODERATOR: Among the four paradoxes listed in the second edition of the Big Book is "We give away to keep." The author defined a paradox as a statement that appears to be false but that, upon examination, can be true in certain instances. "Giving away to keep" certainly sounds like a contradiction, especially because most of us want to improve our material conditions and don't like to give up what we have. But the AA program isn't aimed at persuading people to give up money or material possessions of any kind. Its focus is on giving up self-centeredness by learning to help others and becoming a useful part of the AA community. With this kind of giving, we don't lose anything, but we do gain something.

One thing most of us gain by giving to the program is a great deal of self-worth. We feel good when we're doing something that promotes our common welfare. We will be better people, far better than we were in the wretched self-seeking that accompanied our drinking.

We can also gain more courage in our relationships with others. When we are trying only to be helpful, we lose any fear of being swindled or abused. If others use us to a certain extent, nothing is really lost, because we are giving away to keep. As time passes and we look back on our personal records, we should be able to see that our giving gave us much that we couldn't have gained in any other way.

Who has something to share on this topic?

....

....

....

....

....

....

....

....

....

....

....

....

....

....

Growth through Prayer and Action

● ● ●

MODERATOR: If we are following our program, there should be some kind of real growth in our lives. This comes about by changing the way we think and feel. We also grow by acting differently than we would have acted had we not found the program and its principles.

How do we know when this growth is taking place? One way is to discover that we react differently to situations that used to baffle us. We may still have flashes of resentment and other such problems, but we don't hold on to them, and they no longer destroy us. And growth in sobriety will change a person's appearance to a certain extent. In "The Doctor's Opinion" in the Big Book, the author writes about seeing a man he had treated but being unable to recognize him. The fact is, getting off the booze and the resulting personality change had changed the man so much that the doctor just didn't recognize him. That's a real positive change.

Action in the program means working with others and carrying out our normal duties in the right way. This will bring growth, especially in the way we get along at work and in general society. AA can do all that if we follow the program.

Who has had some experience along this line to share with us?

Happy Coincidences

• • •

MODERATOR: A lot of us have had experiences with "unhappy" coincidences. A typical unhappy coincidence was passing a cop just after we left the bar and were trying to drive with one eye closed. Or another unhappy coincidence was ending up in a relationship with a person who saw from the beginning that he or she could take advantage of us. Some of us seemed to have a built-in radar for attracting the wrong people or situations. What we're looking at now is the possibility of generating coincidences that have happier results. A marvelous coincidence took place back in 1935 when Bill W. made a phone call in Akron that put him in touch with the woman who knew Dr. Bob and also knew of Dr. Bob's desperate efforts to stop drinking. We've heard of many other happy coincidences in AA, and our hope here today is that you might have some to share at this meeting.

Actually, many members say that there are no coincidences or chance occurrences. Everything works according to cause and effect, and if a good or bad coincidence comes into your life, something caused it to happen. And let's face it. When we just happened to pass that cop while we were drunk or just happened to fall for that person who used us, we set ourselves up for this trouble by our own actions.

Working in AA, we can make good things happen if we follow certain principles. The formula is to trust God, clean house, and help others. Doing this, we can clear the deck for better outcomes. Sometimes a seemingly bad break in sobriety can also have good results that surprise us. Can we hear some examples of happy coincidences that came as a result of following the program?

....

....

....

....

....

....

....

....

....

....

....

....

How Do You Think of God?

● ● ●

MODERATOR: We learn in the very beginning of our Twelve Step program that people in AA are encouraged to adopt their own conceptions of God—or Higher Power. This has led to some silly ideas about God. For example, an early AA member was said to believe that his Higher Power was a bus on New York's Fifth Avenue.

AA says it does not offer a conception of God, but we find one in the Big Book, in the chapter titled "We Agnostics." It goes like this: "We found that God does not make too hard terms with those who seek Him. To us, the Realm of Spirit is broad, roomy, all inclusive; never exclusive or forbidding to those who earnestly seek. It is open, we believe, to all men."

What does this tell us? It really says that God is available to all and is not harshly demanding or impossible to please. Many of us were taught that God could never accept us or forgive us. We were so turned off by this conception of God that we turned away from God. We also wondered about the eternal hell that some warned us about. God was supposed to be all-powerful and all-loving, but he had bungled creation so badly that some of his children had to be tortured throughout eternity for their sins here on earth.

Thanks to AA, some of us have been able to establish a conscious contact with God that works for us. We can share with others how we did this. Who would like to start?

....

....

....

....

....

....

....

....

....

....

....

....

....

....

How to Deal with Impatience

• • •

MODERATOR: The topic today, "How to deal with impatience," could just as easily have been "How to find patience." However we phrase it, one of the problems we have in sobriety is developing the patience and perseverance we admire in others but don't have ourselves. You can always get a laugh in meetings by recalling the prayer "Lord, grant me patience, and do it right now!"

It might be unrealistic to believe that alcoholics can be quickly transformed into patient people just by putting down the bottle. Some newcomers display a lot of impatience, for example, in trying to get ahead and rebuild their finances. You hear about people who take two jobs or overwork in some way to repair their financial situations. This can cause setbacks in recovery, because it may mean skipping meetings and building up a lot of unnecessary tension and anxiety.

So what are we to do?

We can start by conceding that we're impatient people who want instant results, instant gratification, instant solutions. But we shouldn't take all the blame for this, because impatience is almost part of the air we breathe. We can get film developed in an hour, an oil change or fast food in minutes, new glasses in an hour, and much more almost instantly. Why should we have to wait for growth and change in the program?

That's where inventory comes in to help us along. By taking an honest inventory, we should be able to see how impatience carries a heavy price. It gives us drive at times, but it can also result in carelessness, mistakes, disappointments, and even tragic accidents. We are the ones who have to look at our own lives to see where we go wrong. One AA member felt that he was schooling himself in patience simply by learning to replace the cap on the toothpaste tube in the morning.

Who can give other examples from personal experience?

How to Keep the Good Tapes

● ● ●

MODERATOR: The Big Book suggests that we should dispose of the wreckage of the past. Closely related to that wreckage are the "old tapes" that play in our heads and give us grief when we should be moving ahead in happy sobriety.

We hear about these old tapes all the time in AA. Members will tell how their parents constantly berated them and predicted that they would never amount to anything. Other old tapes can be about parents fighting or coming home drunk. It's ironic that some children of alcoholics also become alcoholics, even though they grew up resenting the alcoholic behavior of their parents.

But the old tapes aren't all about what happened to us in childhood. Even in AA, we can produce other destructive tapes as we move along. It's very easy to pick up a resentment in the course of a single day and to record it for future playback to remind us how badly we were treated.

The good news in all this is that the tapes we run can be good or bad. If we were recording music or a TV show, we'd quickly delete the things we don't like. We should follow the same rule with the tapes we play in our own heads. We should only play the tapes that make us happy and will have a constructive part in our sobriety.

But how do we do this? That's a good topic for today's discussion. Will a volunteer offer an opinion from personal experience?

How to Find Happy Sobriety

● ● ●

MODERATOR: "How to find happy sobriety" is a good topic for the simple reason that many AA members will frankly admit that they aren't happy all the time. In fact, some people find their sobriety, or at least learn to stay dry, while being miserable much of the time. This doesn't speak well for a program that is supposed to bring peace and serenity.

We know that depression is a major problem for many people in AA. Many of us realize that we were probably using alcohol partly to medicate our depressed moods, which was not a good thing. But even if we aren't terribly depressed, how do we find the happiness so many of us feel we deserve? One way might be to look around at the people who do find happiness in the program—and there are many. Why are they happy and how did they reach that state?

There are three reasons these people are happy: gratitude, acceptance, and service. People who have those three things have a measure of happiness.

Gratitude gets a lot of attention in AA, and it should. Anybody who has found sobriety has escaped a living death and should automatically feel grateful all the time. But we might be fast forgetters as time passes, and we tend to forget the horror we have escaped.

Acceptance means facing reality without self-pity or regret. All of us may have wanted more than we've been able to achieve. But we should not let impossible dreams keep us from being happy with where we are today.

Lastly, there is service, and the people who give it find happiness in the process. The service I'm thinking of is doing things for others, cooperating with others, and working to keep the group going.

Now, who has some additional thoughts on finding happiness?

How Should We Carry the Message?

● ● ●

MODERATOR: Most of us today don't do the one-on-one work that was common for AA members in the early days. We carry the message by attending meetings and being friends and sponsors of others.

But there is still a certain attitude we should have that the pioneering AA members had too. It has to do with how we should carry the message. We should always have an attitude that keeps us from talking down to other alcoholics. If we talk down to people, they will certainly sense it and may reject what we have to say.

Bill W. stated it this way: "Never talk down to an alcoholic from any moral or spiritual hilltop." He added that we should simply lay out the kit of spiritual tools for the alcoholic's inspection. We should show the alcoholic how these tools worked for us and also offer our friendship and fellowship.

It helps to reflect that we are only one drink away from a drunk. The AA program with its spiritual message is our only insurance against taking that drink. So we are really carrying the message for ourselves, whether the other person accepts it or not. If we maintain that attitude, it will help us carry the message in the right way.

Who has some thoughts to add to this?

❶❶❶ MEETING STARTERS

....

....

....

....

....

....

....

....

....

....

....

....

....

....

....

....

Hungry, Angry, Lonely, Tired

● ● ●

MODERATOR: A long time ago, somebody in AA came up with the acronym HALT to stand for *hungry, angry, lonely,* and *tired.* The warning is that when we're in any of these states, we should call a HALT to what we're doing and get back on track with the program.

What's implied here is that alcoholics are people of excess. We can be so busy with something that we fail to eat properly, resulting in unnecessary hunger. Or we can let a resentment get out of hand, allowing anger to overcome us. We can also be so wrapped up in ourselves that we become lonely. And by working or playing too hard, we can be unnecessarily tired. If we reach any of these four states, we are at a greater risk of taking a drink.

When we were drinking, most of us punished ourselves in various ways. We didn't live anything approaching a normal, well-balanced life. It's possible to carry some of those bad habits into sobriety, even without taking a drink.

Along with staying sober, our goal should be to continue building defenses against the difficult emotional states that led to drinking and became part of it. To that end, we should guard against becoming too hungry, angry, lonely, or tired.

Who has been through this experience a num-

ber of times and would like to start a discussion
about it?

....

....

....

....

....

....

....

....

....

....

....

....

....

....

....

....

It's Your Vision That Matters

• • •

MODERATOR: There's a chapter in the Big Book titled "A Vision for You." It ends with this statement: "Abandon yourself to God as you understand God. Admit your faults to Him and to your fellows. Clear away the wreckage of your past. Give freely of what you find and join us. We shall be with you in the Fellowship of the Spirit, and you will surely meet some of us as you trudge the Road of Happy Destiny. May God bless you and keep you—until then."

The important message of this chapter is that the vision of finding a Road of Happy Destiny has to be yours, not another person's. We can tell another person about the program and explain what has happened to change our lives, but that's as far as we can go. People have to visualize themselves as being sober and finding the blessings that they see others enjoying.

While it's only a vision at the time we join the fellowship, we have access to the Power that can make it all come true in our own lives. This is what has really happened countless times in AA. Some people have been in terrible circumstances when they came into AA and have changed their lives in days or months. If you have this vision of finding sobriety and having a better life, you are already well on this Road of Happy Destiny.

One danger, when passing this message on to others, occurs when the person we're trying to help expresses great admiration for what we've found but still holds to the belief that we achieved this only because we have personal strengths that he or she does not possess. If we think people achieve sobriety because of special gifts that we lack, we don't have the right vision. It is very important that we understand the program as a plan that will work for any sincere and honest person.

Maybe this could be a topic for discussion today. May we hear from somebody who finally found sobriety after learning that this vision was for him or her and not just the people who were offering the message?

Justified Resentments

● ● ●

MODERATOR: We've often heard that resentments—deeply held grudges or bottled anger—pose the greatest danger for the recovering alcoholic. We can be doing quite well; we can be having a wonderful day, and then something happens that causes our blood to boil. That's when we can be in danger of taking a drink. If we've been attending meetings and working our program, we should have some defenses when this happens. But that doesn't mean we're home free. Even if the resentment doesn't drive us to the bottle, it can wreck a good day and cause other problems. Under those circumstances, why do we hang on to a resentment?

A big part of the problem is that we may think the resentment is justified. In fact, most resentments *are* justified in the eyes of the people who hold them. Talk to any person who is filled with resentment, and you'll usually get a laundry list of complaints that make it all seem justified.

That doesn't make it right for us. No matter what's been done, the resentment itself is destructive in our own lives. Somebody has said that holding a resentment is like drinking poison and expecting the other person to die. So we are injured twice: first by the action that caused our resentment, and then by the seething rage that clouds our days.

Some of us won't release a resentment because we feel that this is the natural response to whatever injury occurred. Letting go of it, we might think, makes us a doormat. There is also the desire to exact some kind of revenge, though we're not likely to carry it out even if the opportunity comes.

The real victory is to let our resentment go quickly and cleanly, however we're able to do this. And that can be our topic today. How do we deal with resentment when it seems to be justified?

If possible, it would be good to hear from somebody who was able to do just that in a specific case.

Keep It Simple

• • •

MODERATOR: Dr. Bob Smith died more than fifty years ago, but his enduring advice to AA has been "Keep it simple." He went on to say that AA consists of love and service, and we should know what those are. He practiced those in his own life.

"Keep it simple" is a good principle to follow in staying sober. The statement of purpose we read at every meeting makes this point. Our only purpose is to stay sober and help others achieve sobriety. All of us have opinions and affiliations, but these are not part of our program.

We can also improve our lives by practicing simplicity. One of the alcoholic's problems is trying to do too much too soon. Some people get sober, then look at their wretched financial conditions and decide they need to work two jobs. This means cutting down on meetings and taking time and energy away from the program. We also put pressure on ourselves to repair the wreckage of the past. In some cases, that wreckage can never be repaired, and our only course is to make whatever amends are indicated and then move on with living a sober life. We only complicate our lives if we fret about our past mistakes or make useless attempts to recover something that is lost forever. We can simply be grateful that these troubles forced us to seek help.

The AA program is designed to help us simplify our lives. Some people reduce it to three steps: trust God, clean house, and help others. Cleaning house usually means "Keep it simple."

Will somebody start the discussion with a personal example? How does "Keep it simple" work for you?

....

....

....

....

....

....

....

....

....

....

....

....

....

....

Let It Begin with Me

● ● ●

MODERATOR: Today's topic, "Let it begin with me," focuses on our own responsibility. Other people can't stay sober for us.

If we look around in society, we find a lot of people who feel that someone else should take responsibility for them and make things better for them in some magical way. But it was never society's fault that we got drunk and caused trouble for ourselves and others. We were the ones who took that first drink, and we would have resented it if society or anyone else had tried to stop us.

We usually have a part in bringing about whatever happens in our lives. We also have a responsibility to initiate thinking and actions that will bring about our recovery and continue to enhance it. We can do this by doing the following:

1. Accepting the First Step. Admitting that a problem is there and becoming willing to do something about it.
2. Getting to meetings and staying in touch with AA. We can ask others for help with transportation, but it's our responsibility to show up.
3. Taking personal inventory and making our own contact with our Higher Power.

4. Helping others and working on matters that are in the group's interest, because our individual efforts will help determine whether the group lives or dies.

We can also take the AA Responsibility Statement for ourselves: "I am responsible. When anyone, anywhere, reaches out for help, I want the hand of AA always to be there. And for that: I am responsible."

Who can share an example of taking responsibility?

Letting Go of Guilt

●●●

MODERATOR: Alcoholics are frequently accused of thinking only about themselves and being indifferent to the destruction they cause in other people's lives. This may be true of alcoholics while they're still drinking. But good recovery includes feelings of remorse about the wrongs of the past. In fact, it may even be a bad sign if a person has no guilt or remorse about having done things that were obviously harmful.

But we also know that excessive feelings of guilt will hamper our efforts to establish happy sobriety. Some people might not be able to stay sober at all because they wallow in too much guilt. This isn't a good state of affairs at all, and it's something we should work on. The Twelve Step program is a method of dealing with guilt. We can begin by doing a thorough inventory that includes being completely honest about sins of commission and omission—things we've done wrong and things we didn't do that we should have. This is necessary so that we can understand what might be causing our feelings of guilt. We should not suppress the truth, whatever it is.

The next thing we might do is discuss it with our sponsor or another understanding person. We should determine whether amends are necessary or even possible. When it is no longer possible to make amends, it's important to forgive ourselves and to accept the wrongs of the past rather than to continue to beat ourselves up over them. In the meantime, we should also seek God's guidance and forgiveness in the matter. We should continue to do this if the guilt persists. In time, we should find our guilty feelings easing or at least no longer preventing us from functioning as we should.

We are assuming, of course, that the guilt we're talking about concerns our own wrongs. We should not feel guilty about problems we did not cause.

Is there a volunteer who has suggestions for dealing with guilt?

Letting Go of Problems

● ● ●

MODERATOR: One of the slogans used in AA is "Let go and let God." What does this mean and how do we do it?

To get any benefit out of this slogan, it follows that we should at least believe in God or believe that a Higher Power is active in our lives. No rational person could expect any good outcomes from a nonexistent God or a Higher Power that has no place in his or her life. But if we do believe in a Higher Power, certain changes follow this belief.

By changing our thoughts, feelings, and actions, we find our lives changing in what seem to be perfectly natural ways. We find that it's better to let things happen than try to force the outcomes we would like to have. In other words, we may be making our problems worse by trying too hard to solve them in our own way. There might be better outcomes that we haven't even considered.

One AA member wanted to buy a small business, prayed about it, and was rather angry with God when the deal fell through. Just a short time later, however, he found another opportunity that was even better than the one he had failed to get. We might call that an example of our Higher Power working for our highest good.

Many things in life seem to work that way. If

a key gets stuck in a lock, forcing it makes the situation worse. If you're flying an airplane and it stalls, the solution is to release the stick, and the plane rights itself. And if we force people to do things against their will, especially our children, we'll pay a price for it later on. We always have to do our part, and it's obvious that we can't just sit back and expect God to micromanage our lives. But it is a good principle to "Let go and let God." Who will offer some thoughts on how this has worked for him or her?

Life after Cloud Nine

● ● ●

MODERATOR: One common complaint in AA is that we go through an initial period of elation after getting sober and then drop back into a mood of gloom and indifference. That period of elation is called "cloud nine," and most of us wish that we could have something like that forever. However, it doesn't seem to last. We could compare this period to the feeling we get after recovering from an illness such as the flu. We feel three times better the first day, and then the feeling fades and we just feel normal. The truth is that we can't go from day to day experiencing more elation every day.

In fact, that may have been part of the trickery of drinking. There was always going to be some mysterious benefit in the next drink or the next drunk. Some of us even had the weird notion that somewhere down the road we would have a spectacular drunk that would be so marvelous we would never want to drink again! It sounds crazy, but of course the whole drinking experience was crazy.

What we're really facing is that getting sober means getting in touch with reality. And the real world is not arranged so that we can live in continuous ecstasy. The world of reality includes problems, disappointments, boredom, occasional pain, and rejections. There is no cloud nine in the real world.

Our job, as recovering alcoholics, is to face life on life's terms—and that means facing reality. Who will start this discussion with an example from his or her own life?

Live and Let Live

● ● ●

MODERATOR: We see the slogan "Live and let live" posted on lots of meeting-room walls, but what real meaning does it have for us? Can it really make a difference in the way we think and live? It is a good topic for discussion today because so many of us have trouble with other people. We sit in on meetings where people talk about their terrible bosses or the troubles they're having with a spouse or former friend. If you attend enough AA meetings, you'll hear about every human relations problem under the sun.

Before you go out to see a conflict-resolution specialist, however, it might be possible to find an answer in this simple slogan. It conveys several important ideas:

1. Let other people be themselves; we don't have to manage or control anybody.
2. Stop criticizing other people; don't even think about criticizing them. This means giving up the gossip business.
3. Release grudges from the past. This can include the amends-making that we find in Steps Eight and Nine.

There's more to the meaning of "Live and let live." I'd like to ask somebody to begin the discussion, perhaps by relating an incident that helped put this slogan into action.

Mental Depression after Sobriety

● ● ●

MODERATOR: It may come as quite a surprise that many recovering alcoholics are hit with mental depression after achieving continuous sobriety. This can occur even when one is trying to follow the AA program in its entirety.

Why should this be? After all, we're often told that the program should make us happy, joyous, and free. Why isn't this promise met immediately upon our becoming sober? Is there a flaw in the program?

One suggested answer is that alcoholics use alcohol as a form of self-medication. Though alcohol is rightly called a depressant, it actually served as an "upper" for most of us. It lifted us up, carried us out of the doldrums, and removed the feeling that we were inferior and inadequate. It did this only for a short time, of course, and then it left us in worse shape than ever. But we didn't think of that at the moment we took the first drink.

When we accept the AA program, we give up this dubious form of self-medication. We're then forced to face the pain of living as other people do, which includes facing responsibilities and duties that may terrify us. We can no longer escape into the bottle when depression strikes, and this requires us to find new ways of coping with the problem.

AA cofounder Bill W. suffered from what was

probably deep depression long after achieving sobriety. He struggled to find answers for years, but in the meantime he found that physical activity such as walking helped him survive the times when he was all but paralyzed by depression. He also believed that depression cures itself over time if one stays the course and does not drink.

There are other things to be said about depression, which is a topic we should approach with great humility, knowing that pat answers will not meet every person's need. In the meantime, who has personal experience to share about depression in sobriety?

Needing the Program versus Wanting It

● ● ●

MODERATOR: When we are first introduced to AA and find a new life in the program, we are tempted to suggest it to our old drinking pals who seem to need it. We learn quickly that there is a difference between needing the program and wanting it. We even hear the saying "AA is not for those who need it; it is for those who want it."

Statistics tell us that there are hundreds of thousands of alcoholics out there who ought to consider finding recovery. They seem to need recovery. But they don't feel they need it, and for this reason they can't be reached.

There are ways to get through to people who obviously need the program but aren't ready to want it badly enough. Intervention is one way, although this is not an AA-sponsored practice. Intervention does appear to work when there is some leverage over the alcoholic. It can help, for example, to have an employer who tells you that your job is on the line.

It often takes trouble of some kind to convince alcoholics that they need help. We can begin to want help when we're on the street, in jail, or facing the consequences of an accident or a drink-induced illness.

Most of us agree that we can do little to speed up the process of convincing alcoholics that they need help. Our personal stories can help, however, by showing the contrast between the hellish lives we once had and what our lives became after we found AA. It is even possible for some alcoholics to catch this vision of a better life before they go all the way on the path to destruction.

Who will begin the discussion by sharing some insight on this topic?

....

....

....

....

....

....

....

....

....

....

....

Old Resentments Flaring Up

• • •

MODERATOR: We're supposed to clean house when we come into AA. This means dumping all of our resentments, forgiving ourselves and others for mistakes of the past, and setting out on a new basis for living. This is really the way to happiness, although we usually don't know it until the process has been completed. When it's properly done, however, we will look back on the old thinking and wonder how we survived with it.

Despite this thorough housecleaning, however, old resentments can flare up with a vengeance. This can often occur when we're feeling a touch of envy or when things just haven't gone our way. It can be disturbing to find an old resentment churning up just when we thought it had been eliminated forever.

We can handle an old resentment in the same way we deal with a new one. When it comes up, we immediately recognize it as an old enemy that we thought was a friend. So we dismiss it and refuse to blame ourselves because it flared up. We ask God for the power to rise above it and to return to the peace and serenity that we experience when we're not feeling resentment. The sooner we do this, the better off we'll be. Author Emmet Fox used the example of a person who is standing in front of a fireplace when a sudden spark flies up and lands on his clothes. If he brushes it away immediately, no harm is done. But let the spark stay there, and damage is done. It's the same way with resentment. Let it stay in our thinking, and it causes damage of some kind. And who receives the damage? We do, of course.

Who has an experience to share about an old resentment flaring up?

Principles before Personalities

● ● ●

MODERATOR: The Twelve Traditions don't usually make good meeting topics, but the one exception is Tradition Twelve, which states that anonymity is the spiritual foundation of our traditions and that we need to place principles before personalities. This suggests that we should do the very thing that runs against what people usually do in the larger society: we should always be looking for the principle involved and not let ourselves be influenced by charming and prominent people.

And the influential, wealthy people who belong to AA are not to be counted as more important than any other AA member. Beyond that, we should also be careful not to let ourselves be swayed by people with strong personalities. It is always a matter of *what* is right and not *who* is right.

This idea is hard to grasp because most of us have been conditioned to respond to the personalities among us. The Oxford Group, AA's predecessor society, often relied on prominent people to carry its message and convince others to follow it. Why shouldn't the same idea work in AA?

Actually, the Oxford Group offered the best reason for being careful about personalities. The founder of the group made some ill-advised public statements that seriously damaged the group's effectiveness in the late 1930s. A strong personality can help us, but that same personality also might hurt us.

The truth is, a person with lots of influence and charm does not have the power to keep any of us sober. We get sober and stay that way by following the principles we've been given, not by following any particular person. People can give us the message, but it is then up to us to apply it in our own lives. And the same people who brought us the message of sobriety might eventually falter themselves.

Who would like to pick up on this for further discussion?

Resent Someone

● ● ●

MODERATOR: We are told again and again in AA that resentment is the number one offender—that alcoholics can't really survive if they continue to hold festering resentments. Here is something that explains why resentment is so bad. It's titled "Resent Someone," and it doesn't appear to have a known author.

The moment you start to resent a person, you become his slave. He controls your dreams, absorbs your digestion, robs you of your peace of mind and goodwill, and takes away the pleasure of your work. He ruins your religion and nullifies your prayers. You cannot take a vacation without his going along. He destroys your freedom of mind and hounds you wherever you go. There is no way to escape the person you resent. He is with you when you are awake. He invades your privacy when you sleep. He is close beside you when you drive your car and when you are on the job. You can never have efficiency or happiness. He influences even the tone of your voice. He requires you to take medicine for indigestion, headaches, and loss of energy. He even steals your last moment of consciousness before you go to sleep. So—if you want to be a slave—harbor your resentments!

Who would like to start the discussion by adding to this?

....

....

....

....

....

....

....

....

....

....

....

....

....

....

Responsibilities in Sobriety

● ● ●

MODERATOR: Here's a question we might ask ourselves: "Now that I'm sober, what are my responsibilities?"

AA actually has a Responsibility Statement, which is included in every issue of the *AA Grapevine.* It reads: "I am responsible. When anyone, anywhere, reaches out for help, I want the hand of AA always to be there. And for that: I am responsible."

We could question the wording of this, because it's obvious that none of us as individuals can be responsible for seeing that the hand of AA is available everywhere. We don't have that power, so what's being expressed here is an ideal—something we'd like to see but that is beyond our current resources.

What we can do, however, is provide the hand of AA where we are and where we can be effective. That means keeping AA strong and active in our own group and in our own community. It can also include supporting the larger mission of AA, such as the World Services operations.

What we're really doing in taking on such responsibility is ensuring that the same help that was given to us will be available for others. In carrying out these responsibilities, we'll also be reinforcing our own sobriety.

Some people, of course, don't want to accept these responsibilities. That is their right, and we should not nag them about it. There are others, however, who view this service as a privilege and a delight.

Can we hear from one of you now?

Should We Have the Four Absolutes?

• • •

MODERATOR: It doesn't happen often, but occasionally an AA speaker will bring up the Four Absolutes with the recommendation that we try to follow them.

The Four Absolutes, if you're not familiar with them, are honesty, purity, unselfishness, and love. They're still remembered by some AA members and groups because they had a place in the start of our movement. The Oxford Group used the Four Absolutes, but our later AA literature did not include them. The AA Cleveland Central Office, however, publishes a booklet describing them.

Bill W. insisted that the AA program covers the Four Absolutes without naming them. But since there were good reasons for separating from the Oxford Group in the late 1930s, we might also conclude that eliminating the Absolutes was a deliberate move to distance the AA fellowship from its parent society. Bill felt that the Oxford Group was falling fast in the public favor, and any identification with it would have been too much baggage for the fledgling society of AA. He also said that *absolute* was too strong a term for us.

But some people called the Four Absolutes the "Four Standards" instead. This makes it more acceptable for us. Maybe we should talk about it today.

Who wants to address this question: Would it help us as individuals to have Four Standards called honesty, purity, unselfishness, and love?

Surrender to Win

● ● ●

MODERATOR: A previous edition of the Big Book carried an interesting article about four paradoxes that apply to AA. One is called "Surrender to win." The author defined a paradox as a statement that appears to be false but that, upon examination, can be true in certain instances.

"Surrender to win" certainly sounds like a contradiction because we link surrender to defeat. We also place a high value on winning at any cost, and we hate to be labeled as losers. *Loser,* in fact, is a term we use for a person who is failing at everything.

But in AA we have winners—and these are the very people who made the kind of surrender that's necessary for getting sober and staying that way. These winners admitted complete defeat in the drinking game; they gave up completely and continue to admit that they can't take one drink without getting into very serious trouble. This is not an easy admission to make for people whose lives are built around drinking.

That very surrender, however, opens the door to things that were never possible in the old life. We begin to win back things that alcohol had stolen from us, and life becomes filled with new possibilities. But we are winners only because we surrendered the drinking problem.

A number of other things ought to be surrendered in order to win, but they are always things that are not worth keeping: false pride, lying, fear, pretensions, and self-seeking—all the things that go along with active alcoholism.

Can we hear something from a winner about the process of surrendering?

Taking the Tenth Step

● ● ●

MODERATOR: The Tenth Step of the AA program is "Continued to take personal inventory and when we were wrong promptly admitted it." You could call this Step the eraser on the pencil. It allows us to eliminate the mistakes and start over.

The Tenth Step serves such a good purpose, so why is it so hard for many of us to take it? Why do we continue to hold on to wrong thoughts or defend actions that will only be harmful in the long run? The answer must be that we have a human need to defend our positions, even when we are wrong. There is probably a false belief that if we refuse to admit when we're wrong, the mistake will go away or correct itself. And of course, we can sometimes bully people into doing things our way even when we're wrong.

We are able to get past this problem if we're really sincere about what we're trying to do in AA. We are trying to live in peace with ourselves and others, we are trying to make progress in our personal lives, and we are trying to use our own resources and skills to the best advantage. We can't do any of these things if we're not willing to face our mistakes and correct them.

AA cofounder Bill W. liked to use business examples to show how the program works. He would say that a business that does not take frequent inventory will go broke. The purpose of a business inventory is to identify the things that won't sell, get rid of them, and go on to stock items that will make money for the business. In our own lives, we need to get rid of the thoughts and actions that cause trouble. We must then take on new ideas and practices that will benefit us and others.

Who has some experience to share on this topic?

....

....

....

....

....

....

....

....

....

....

....

The ABCs of AA

• • •

MODERATOR: The fifth chapter of the Big Book, "How It Works," contains three statements that could be called the ABCs of AA. They are read at every meeting, but I'll repeat them here. They are (a) That we were alcoholic and could not manage our own lives; (b) That probably no human power could have relieved our alcoholism; and (c) That God could and would if He were sought.

These are powerful statements that will save our lives if they are accepted and believed wholeheartedly. In fact, these three things are probably all we need to know to get a firm start in AA.

But why is it hard for so many people to grasp the ABCs? Well, to begin with, it takes real honesty to accept that first statement—that we were alcoholic and could not manage our own lives. We have to give up forever the idea that we'll ever be able to take one drink safely. And there may be people telling us that we're not really alcoholic and can recover control.

As for the second statement, we should have pretty much lost confidence in any human power to help us. Nobody can stay sober for us, and our own powers have proved to be inadequate for the task.

The third statement, "God could and would if He were sought," requires us to believe that there is a Higher Power who can and will help us. But do we really believe that?

Who will start the discussion by sharing an account of his or her struggles with these statements?

....

....

....

....

....

....

....

....

....

....

....

....

....

....

....

The Fear of Rejection

● ● ●

MODERATOR: It hardly needs saying that the typical alcoholic will face lots of rejection, if only because of drinking problems. But rejection doesn't go away just because we've stopped drinking. Rejection is part of living, and our challenge is to accept it and deal with it constructively.

What we have to deal with in sobriety might be called "the fear of rejection." Rejection itself is so painful and devastating that we don't even face situations in which there is a risk of being rejected. These situations might involve calling on prospective customers, applying for a job, asking for a date, or getting involved in almost anything where we might lose out.

If we allow the fear of rejection to take over and dominate our lives, we are in effect sabotaging ourselves and destroying opportunities for future success and happiness. So how can we rise above this problem and put it behind us?

The Serenity Prayer gives us a clue. We can ask God for the courage to change the things we can. And of course one of the things we want to change is any fear that keeps us from acting in our own best interests.

We must also understand that we risk rejection even when the chances of success seem to be fairly high. But this shouldn't prevent us from taking the risk. Any success will give us the confidence to move ahead into more activities that we would like to pursue. It will also help to talk to our friends about our fears about rejection. We must understand that every person in the world has to face rejection at some point. Successful people are those who don't take rejection personally unless it really is personal. And even if the rejection is personal, the correct response is to shrug it off and go on with our lives.

It is also helpful to know that God is in charge of our lives and that rejection sometimes works to point us in the right direction. In any case, who has a comment on this topic?

The Importance of Continuing

● ● ●

MODERATOR: In the old Oxford Group that supplied AA's major principles, continuance—basically, the ability to stick with something—was an important part of the program. It was understood that merely accepting and practicing something for the short term didn't really work over time. To benefit from the program, the group members knew that you had to stay with it, to persevere no matter what was going on.

Our AA experience should tell us the same thing. Many people come to the fellowship, seem temporarily dazzled by our program, and then quit after a short time. Not surprisingly, they don't get much out of it. We even hear them say that they tried AA and it didn't work for them.

It didn't work because AA is an ongoing program that works one day at a time. It's what we're thinking and doing today that really counts, and continuance means doing this every day for years and years. Every old-timer in the program, for example, put it all together only one day at a time. It is true that over time in the program we should develop new habits and strengths of character that will sustain us in times of distress. But we can't project today's thinking into the future, and we don't seem to be able to store up whatever it is that keeps us sober.

We can't decide today how we'll be thinking and acting in the future. If we drink, of course, all bets for the future are off. But if we accept continuance as a vital factor in our program, we'll be more likely to succeed in the days and years ahead. So, just as we tell people to "Think, think, think," we should also remind them to "Continue, continue, continue."

Who will open the discussion with thoughts on continuance?

The Need for Self-Honesty

• • •

MODERATOR: We hear at almost every AA meeting that the most troubled people can recover from alcoholism if they have the capacity to be honest. We should also learn that what's meant here is being honest with ourselves.

AA cofounder Bill W. talked about this often. In the little book *As Bill Sees It*, he says that the deception of others is nearly always rooted in the deception of ourselves. In other words, find a person who is generally dishonest, and you'll also have a person who has little self-honesty. You'll find that person blaming others for his troubles and believing that with just a little good luck, he'll be able to turn his life around with no soul-searching or change on his part.

We don't have to look in prisons or asylums for such people, because many of us have been more or less afflicted by this same problem, especially with regard to drinking. The typical alcoholic goes through a period of believing that he or she can recover control even when all the signs are saying that it's never going to work. Trouble will eventually drive us into facing the problem honestly, but sometimes it takes a long time.

When honesty is discussed, we hear some people quickly assert that we're not talking about "cash-register honesty." Are they really saying that it's still okay to be dishonest in money matters even while trying to stay sober in AA? Some people have even said, "You might still be a burglar after you join AA, but at least you'll be a sober burglar!" We can hardly agree that *this* is real honesty! Maybe there are other opinions around the table. Who will be the first to explain why self-honesty is important?

Tricky Comparisons

● ● ●

MODERATOR: Sometimes we get what seem to be mixed messages in AA. We're advised to learn from the experience of others, and yet we're warned not to compare. We get such warnings because making comparisons can be tricky and may lead us to think we don't have a drinking problem.

We should be careful about comparisons when hearing a very hard story from a person who has endured terrible things. We could easily use such an example to decide that we aren't alcoholics, because none of these things happened to us. All kinds of behaviors are represented in the fellowship. Some people drifted to skid row, others committed crimes, and still others were terribly neglectful of their real responsibilities. Yet we have many members whose drinking was so concealed that even their closest friends didn't really know they were alcoholic.

AA is a large umbrella that can cover many kinds of drinkers. The common factor is that we are powerless over alcohol, and it has made our lives unmanageable. If we are not really powerless and our lives are not unmanageable, then we don't belong in AA.

But that is a determination that only the individual should make. Instead of making tricky comparisons with others, we should look at what alcohol is doing to us and decide for ourselves if we need the program. If any of us have real drinking problems, we belong in AA.

I would now invite someone to share how making comparisons turned out to be tricky, and also how you worked your way out of it.

Trouble in Finding a Higher Power

● ● ●

MODERATOR: Large numbers of AA members tell us that in the beginning they had trouble with the concept of a Higher Power. Some of this stemmed from resentment over the way God was presented to them while they were growing up. Others feel that the universe exists but has no need for a centralized God who oversees everything. Bill W. wrote the following about his own feelings, "I resisted the thought of a Czar of the heavens, however loving His sway might be." But Bill W. did find a Higher Power in his life and managed to put together the basics of the AA program, though he often admitted that he had great personal shortcomings. He never tried to impose his religious views on the rest of us. His fundamental belief about the role of a Higher Power in AA could be summed up in these three points made in "How It Works," the fifth chapter of the Big Book: (a) That we were alcoholic and could not manage our own lives; (b) That probably no human power could have relieved our alcoholism; (c) That God could and would if He were sought.

We realize we are whipped and that we can tap into a Higher Power that has apparently worked for others.

We should admit, however, that even this simple formula gives some of us problems. Who will offer some information about getting over this hurdle?

Truth and Honesty

● ● ●

MODERATOR: We often hear about the HOW of the AA program, which is *honesty, open-mindedness,* and *willingness.* Honesty is the first of these three, so it comes across as a good topic for discussion today. What is honesty in AA terms? We sometimes hear that we're not talking about "cash-register honesty" here; in other words, stealing is not the major problem. But of course we should include cash-register honesty because good AA practice should not gloss over crime. We should strive for honesty in all things.

The really big hurdle is in learning to be honest with oneself. Once we deal with self-honesty, monetary honesty should no longer be a problem. But three barriers are in our way to self-honesty: pride, fear, and self-deception. Self-deception may be the highest barrier, because alcoholism itself is a process of self-deception. We consistently deceived ourselves about what we were doing when we drank—that we were doing something destructive while looking for favorable outcomes. As long as we continued in this self-deceptive mode, we continued to have trouble.

But pride and fear are also problems. There is the false pride of being forced to recognize that we aren't what we've pretended to be. There is also the fear of being found out, of being discovered for what we really are.

How do we get past these barriers? That's what we want to find out today. Who has had an experience with this that can be shared at this meeting?

Walk in Dry Places

● ● ●

MODERATOR: Why should we stay in "dry" places when we're trying to stay sober in AA? The Big Book tells us it's okay to have lunch with a friend in a bar if we're spiritually sound. If that's okay, why isn't it also okay to go into the bar just to see friends and hang out for a while?

Some people probably do, but it's not recommended as good practice. The main reason is that selling alcoholic drinks is the principal business of the bar, and most people go there to drink and not just hang out. When you go into a bar for soft drinks, you're not really helping to pay the rent or the bartenders' salaries. There are other places to go for a soft drink.

We also have to look at our own motives carefully. If we go into bars frequently, there must be some desire to retain that old drinking lifestyle. We might be wishing to return to that life and secretly hoping that we can do it without the pain and suffering we previously encountered. That's not in the cards, of course, but sometimes our alcoholic fantasies die hard.

Another point is that sober living should include building a new social life with different friends. Some people think it's wrong to desert our old drinking pals, but the truth is, they'll desert us when they learn we're not drinking anymore. Drinking friendships are not the solid friendships we need in our new life.

There are also special categories of wet places, such as weddings, anniversary parties, and business cocktail parties. AA friends can tell us how to deal with these.

Everything I've said so far is just opinion. I'd like to throw the topic out on the table now and see who runs with it.

Wanting Instant Gratification

● ● ●

MODERATOR: Now and then we hear a person say, "I want what I want when I want it." This is the person who wants instant gratification for everything, and it's a typical problem with alcoholics. We're not the only people who want what we want when we want it. You can see it in our commercial world, where we have instant oil changes, fast-food outlets, one-hour photo processing, and many other things on a quickie basis. This idea may be beneficial when it comes to goods and services, but it's destructive when applied to alcoholism.

Drinking always helped us get out of whatever mood we were in, come to terms with wherever we were, and deal with both success and failure. It was the instant painkiller for the emotions that dogged us.

In getting sober, we have to part company with this old friend called alcohol. This is not an easy separation because it means giving up the instant solutions that alcohol seemed to provide. We have to go it alone—without alcohol—and we have to face the fact that we can't get what we want every time we want it. The answer, as we're often told in AA, is to live life on life's terms. We have to accept the slow progress and the steady improvement that other people are willing to accept. We may always want the quick fix, but we can learn that it has its harmful side.

Who can give us some insight on this problem?

....

....

....

....

....

....

....

....

....

....

....

....

....

....

We Cannot Live with Anger

● ● ●

MODERATOR: Bottled-up anger, which we also call resentment, is considered one of the alcoholic's most serious problems. It can take many forms and pop up when we least expect it. Being sober in AA isn't always a protection from anger, nor do we ever seem to be completely free from it. But we can at least work on it.

Marty M. was one of the first women to find sobriety in AA. She was a strong, intelligent person who had dealt with lots of problem people in her life. And usually, when she became angry at somebody, she could handle it aggressively and in her own way. But then something happened that angered her, and she couldn't do a single thing about it. This was in the very early days of AA, when she was trying to grasp the essentials of the program. She was angry at somebody, but there wasn't any way that she could get back at him.

While her rage was consuming her, a sentence came into her mind that she must have heard in AA: "We cannot live with anger." It had a profound effect on her as she realized how true the statement was. We can be angry, but it will kill us. It is, after all, one of the deadly sins, something that can be lethal in the extreme. Her response was to turn it over to her Higher Power in prayer. It worked, and she went on to do great work in the field of alcoholism. Years later, she would still be sharing this experience with other AA members.

Has anyone at the table had a similar experience in dealing with anger? Would you be willing to share an experience of your own that helped you make peace with it?

....

....

....

....

....

....

....

....

....

....

....

....

....

We Die to Live

● ● ●

MODERATOR: The second edition of the Big Book featured a story titled "The Professor and the Paradox," which introduced four paradoxes in connection with AA and recovery. The author defined a paradox as a statement that appears to be false but that, upon examination, can be true in certain instances. One of these four paradoxes is "We die to live."

This is a startling idea because death and dying seem to be the end of life. If we lose our own identities and conscious existence, what do we have left?

But the author in this story is talking about another kind of death, which is giving up the old person we were and being born into a new way of life. It is probably the AA version of being born again.

Most of the AA stories we hear at open "lead" meetings are really accounts of this process of being born again. There is the old person of the drinking life, trapped in a web of beliefs, desires, ideas, and emotions that caused endless trouble. There seemed to be no way out of this enslavement. And there was no way out for the old person whose identity was built around all of the destructive ideas and beliefs that were killing him or her.

This old personality must be given up in order to find the new life in AA. A new foundation for living must be put in place, which then has the effect of making us people who think differently and behave differently. This is dying in order to live.

We won't know what really happens in physical death until the time comes for each of us. But our experience shows that giving up the old person and being born again in AA is the way to a new life.

Who has experience to share on this topic?

What about My Old Friends?

• • •

MODERATOR: You don't have to be in AA very long before you hear a newcomer ask how he or she should relate to old friends. Time and again, we hear people fret about this, sometimes mentioning people they like very much but who are still drinking. AA does not ask anybody to drop old friends. But it does suggest that our number one goal is to stay sober at all costs and to take any and all steps that are needed to maintain sobriety. By staying sober, we can be in a position to set other priorities as they appear.

We need to be honest about the nature of our old friendships. If they were all built on drinking, we don't have to drop these friends. They will probably drop us when they realize we won't drink with them anymore. Our real friends, however, will be glad that we're doing something to straighten out our lives. We also have to remember that alcohol is the old friend that wants to call us back whenever possible. If we're not really honest, we may go back to old friends when our real motive is to drink again.

We can promise that anybody who is worried about losing friends will be able to make many new ones in AA. We have friendships that have lasted decades. AA lives on friendships, and some members even call themselves "friends of Bill W." Another good idea is to "walk in dry places." This means staying out of bars, even if we don't plan to drink alcohol there. If we're spiritually sound, we can have lunch with friends in bars or attend cocktail parties, but sobriety must come first. Any practice or any relationship that threatens sobriety ought to be questioned. But give AA a chance, and the friendships will work out in the right way.

Now, who will start the discussion by bringing up a time when this seemed to be a problem?

What Blocks Acceptance?

• • •

MODERATOR: One of the questions we should ask ourselves now and then is "What blocks acceptance?" in regard to our drinking. Why is it so difficult to convince ourselves and others that we are alcoholic and need AA's help? With any other kind of affliction, people are usually grateful for help as soon as it is offered. But alcoholism is not that way. Many come to look AA over, but few stay to find real sobriety.

I can offer a few thoughts as moderator, but I hope we'll find others in our discussion. The best place to start is to recall our own thoughts and feelings before we decided to accept the AA program. What was going on in our lives that made it difficult for us to reach out for help? What attitudes might have gotten in the way?

One of the first hurdles is false pride. Once safely in the program, we easily forget how prideful alcoholics can be while they're still drinking. We hate to admit that we are powerless over a substance that has seemed so dear to us. It makes us feel vulnerable and weak. It's like the fear of being stripped naked in public.

And giving up alcohol may also feel like we're being left naked, with nothing to support us. Alcohol has been an old friend, though definitely a treacherous one. And like an old friend, it can still call to us persistently, inviting us to come back.

It may also be difficult to visualize a life without alcohol, not realizing that we're really being given a chance to live a decent life after years of hell. We may see others enjoying the benefits of AA but not believe that we can have the same benefits by accepting the program.

Who will share experience on this subject?

What Is a Principle?

● ● ●

MODERATOR: The Twelfth Step in the AA program refers to the previous Steps as principles. *Principle* is a term we take for granted. What is a principle, and how can we benefit by having a set of principles for living?

One definition of a principle is that it's "a fundamental guide to action." This guide will tell us how to act in situations that come up. If similar situations come up repeatedly, a person of principle will usually respond in the same way each time. A principle isn't always a good thing. It can be said that most alcoholics have a principle of using alcohol to deal with various situations, such as when celebrating or when dealing with a disappointment or a setback. Some alcoholics also have a principle of lying when the truth might serve them better.

We should develop *good* principles when we're practicing the program. One good principle is that we don't drink, no matter what happens—whether we suffer a devastating loss or win the lottery. Another principle is that we don't lie or cheat, and we take special care not to harm other people.

A most important principle is taking matters to our Higher Power and expecting guidance as we go along in life. As we learn to do this, we discover a fundamental guide to action that will serve us well in the long run.

Growth in the program should mean a continuous process of learning better principles and acting according to them. Who has some experience along this line to share?

....

....

....

....

....

....

....

....

....

....

....

....

....

What Is Being Spiritually Fit?

● ● ●

MODERATOR: According to the Big Book, if we are spiritually fit, we can do all sorts of things alcoholics are not supposed to do. This includes going into bars and attending events where alcoholic drinks are served. It may even include keeping liquor in one's home to serve to nonalcoholic friends. But there is a danger that some people might not understand what "spiritually fit" means. If we get into drinking situations for the wrong reasons, we are setting ourselves up for trouble. Our motive for dropping into bars just to see our old friends from our drinking days might really be a hidden desire to live that drinking life again. We might be trying to recapture whatever it was we thought we were getting from drinking.

Being spiritually fit includes having contact with a Higher Power that protects and guides us in all sorts of situations and environments. However, we should also be conscious of the need to do our part in cleaning house, taking inventory, and understanding why we are taking certain actions. We should have legitimate reasons for being in situations where alcohol is involved. A business lunch or a family wedding is usually a legitimate reason, but our own house should be in order as we move into these situations. We should never gamble with our sobriety.

If we are spiritually fit, we understand that we have a strong desire to stay sober under any and all conditions. No amount of liquor can get us drunk until we take that fatal first drink. Understanding that, we can safely navigate our way through all kinds of social situations without harm.

Who has had experience to share on this topic?

....

....

....

....

....

....

....

....

....

....

....

....

What Is Insanity?

● ● ●

MODERATOR: The AA pioneers really threw us a fastball when they inserted the phrase "restore us to sanity" in the Twelve Steps. This suggests that we apparently were insane, despite how well we may have been managing some parts of our lives. We hear people say that insanity is doing the same thing over and over while expecting a better outcome the next time. That's what happens with alcoholics. No matter how much trouble we cause, there's the frantic hope that things will be different the next time around. But they aren't; the insane behavior repeats itself endlessly.

Insanity isn't the goofy or tragic behavior that we exhibit while drunk. The insanity is in taking a first drink even when the grim record already shows that it's going to be disastrous.

What does it take to make this admission that we were insane? A strong desire to recover can be a powerful tool. It's also helpful to get rid of the false pride that makes us think we're still different from the people who have gone before us in AA.

But if we must admit that we've been insane, the good news is that we can recover. All we have to do is stay away from the first drink and change the wretched ideas and beliefs that have kept us trapped in the vicious cycle. Of course, this isn't as simple as it sounds. But with support in AA, we don't have to stay insane.

May we have a volunteer who will offer some personal thoughts on the nature of insanity—that is, the insanity of the practicing alcoholic?

What Is Living One Day at a Time?

• • •

MODERATOR: The idea of living one day at a time has been with AA almost from the beginning. What it means is that we can stay sober by not trying to live our whole lives at once. If we think about not having a drink for the rest of our lives, the thought of sobriety becomes overwhelming.

In a sick way, alcoholics who are still drinking tend to live one day at a time. If there is enough money or booze to last through the day, an alcoholic usually does not worry about facing the horrible truth tomorrow.

In sobriety, the same idea can be used in a healthy way. We can confidently state that we can and will stay sober for the present day, come what may. At the same time, we can be realistic about what we should focus on in the use of our time and thought for the present day. Regrets from the past and fears for the future can intrude on living in the present day, but they should be rigorously dismissed.

On the other hand, our responsibilities today may involve repairing something in our past or planning for the future. But these duties should be met without any hand-wringing or worry. If we take out a mortgage, for example, we're assuming an obligation that may go on for years. Actions such as these fall in the category of calculated risks, and we should have already determined that we will be able to meet these obligations under normal conditions and especially if we stay sober.

Staying sober today should also mean thinking in a sober way for today. It is dangerous for an alcoholic to stay sober for today but be thinking about getting drunk in the future. Who will start the discussion by giving a personal understanding of letting "One day at a time" work in sobriety?

....

....

....

....

....

....

....

....

....

....

....

....

What Is Open-Mindedness?

● ● ●

MODERATOR: We are told that the HOW of the AA program includes *honesty, open-mindedness,* and *willingness,* but what do these terms really mean? What's needed for real open-mindedness, the second item in HOW?

If we have been honest, we already know that we considered ourselves to be open-minded even while we were still drinking. Some of us may have even prided ourselves on being nonjudgmental. Let's be even more honest and admit that we wanted to be open-minded about our drinking activities, and we wanted people to be nonjudgmental about our wrongs. The bargain was that we would withhold judgment on others who might be guilty of certain wrongs.

The open-mindedness we should be looking for in the program is toward new ideas that we wouldn't have previously considered. We don't have to accept every idea that comes down the road, but we surely ought to consider ideas that have some promise of being able to help us. If we completely shut our minds to the possibility that we can be helped, we might be signing our own death warrants.

A marvelous quote in the Big Book is attributed to Herbert Spencer. Whatever its source, it fits our situation: "There is a principle which is a bar against all information, which is proof against all arguments and which cannot fail to keep a man in everlasting ignorance—that principle is contempt prior to investigation." Open-mindedness is just the opposite—a readiness to investigate any ideas that might help us. Who has experience to share on this subject?

What Is Prayer and Meditation?

● ● ●

MODERATOR: We've picked a topic today that focuses on the Eleventh Step: seeking through prayer and meditation the knowledge of God's will for us, and also seeking the power to carry it out. Obviously, we can't do something unless we have the necessary power to do it.

Prayer and meditation are experienced by each of us individually and are shaped by all of our previous notions about God, prayer, religion, and our own place in the world. Time and again we hear people in AA say that they have been scared off by notions of a punishing God that they learned about in their early religious training. Others are skeptical that anybody "up there" is listening. It certainly is fair to ask why we should pray to a Higher Power if we don't even believe that there's any power there to communicate with.

Do prayer and meditation work? If you read the AA literature, beginning with Bill's story in the Big Book, you'll find people saying that it does. What they're saying is that nothing worked until they found a Higher Power in their lives and learned how to make conscious contact with this Higher Power on a regular basis. But others will sneer at this. They doubt this so much that they will not even try it. And of course, if they have this attitude, there's not much we can do to help them.

Others will also insist that we must follow specific beliefs and practices, which they outline for us. We are under no obligation to accept anybody's specific beliefs. All we ask is respect for one another and a willingness to live together in harmony on a spiritual basis.

At this time, I'd like to present the question "What is prayer and meditation?" Who will offer his or her views from personal experience?

What Is Sincerity?

● ● ●

MODERATOR: The first big hurdle we have to clear in the program is the First Step—having a sincere desire to stop drinking. This is no easy thing because it means giving up someone we long regarded as a good old friend. At one time, this good old friend was called John Barleycorn, and he seemed to solve all of our problems, at least temporarily. But he betrayed and enslaved us, and now we have to break free.

If we are sincere in wanting to part with this old friend, we will be willing to resist all of his efforts to re-enslave us. We will give up anything that seems to be too closely associated with drinking, especially the habit of visiting bars just to meet old companions. We won't flirt with any practice that gets us back into the world of drinking.

Sometimes we hear AA members mention how much they wanted a cold beer on a hot day. But if we're sincere about giving up alcohol, we'll recognize this as a faint but persistent desire to drink. After all, on any hot day when we're thirsty, we can choose from a large assortment of cold beverages that do not contain alcohol. Members also express fear about attending family gatherings that involve alcohol. But if we really mean business about staying sober, no such event can really threaten our sobriety.

Sincerity, in AA, is a deep feeling way down inside that tells us we can and will stay sober at all costs, come what may. If we have this, we can accept the First Step and pass into other phases of the program.

All the water in the ocean can't sink a ship unless it gets inside. And all the alcohol in the world can't get us drunk unless we take a drink.

Who has a thought to share about the topic of sincerity?

....

....

....

....

....

....

....

....

....

....

....

What Is Willingness?

● ● ●

MODERATOR: We hear often that willingness is the key to success in AA. It is the third item in the HOW of the program: honesty, open-mindedness, and willingness. How can we develop the kind of willingness that is necessary to accept the program and continue in it?

One of the first things to remember is that all of us have free will, even in the depths of our despair. We can still make certain choices that will have a bearing on our future well-being. We can decide to accept the program or reject it. We can come up with all kinds of reasons why the program will not work for us. And we can praise others for their success in staying sober but still choose to think that it cannot work for us.

Another thought is that willingness usually comes when we want something bad enough. If we were drowning, we would be immediately willing to grab on to anything that might save us. If we really want to save our lives, we should be willing to consider what the program offers us and follow through with it.

We all have the ability to generate willingness. We were willing to make plenty of sacrifices to keep drinking. We sometimes put up with humiliation and loss just to maintain our drinking habits.

Sometimes we even had to swallow pride to keep on drinking. At every meeting, we get advice to practice willingness—but this time, it's willingness to stay sober. Our Big Book says, "If you have decided you want what we have and are willing to go to any length to get it—then you are ready to take certain steps."

Who will start the discussion with some comments about personal difficulty in finding willingness?

What's Needed for Staying Sober

● ● ●

MODERATOR: Every now and then, somebody warns us that we need to get back to basics. The basic issue for an alcoholic is learning what's needed to stay sober. We should always talk about that when there's a new member at the meeting. It's also good to remind ourselves frequently of this basic question: What do I need to know or do to stay sober?

Most AA members will say immediately that we need to accept the First Step and continue to believe it—that we are powerless over alcohol. It is very dangerous to entertain the idea that someday we might be able to drink safely. This just isn't in the cards for an alcoholic, but there is a danger that this idea might be lurking somewhere in our thinking. If it's there, it ought to be rooted out at all costs.

We also believe in taking certain actions, such as attending meetings, taking personal inventory, and staying out of "wet places" where alcohol or the pressure to drink might be present. It's true that some of us can hardly avoid such places due to our work. But if we have to spend some time in wet places, we must at least see to it that our thinking isn't wet. The Big Book tells us that we can be in such places if we are on sound spiritual grounds.

We should be relieved to know that we don't need complicated psychological knowledge or other information in order to stay sober. The Big Book sums it up neatly: (a) That we were alcoholic and could not manage our own lives; (b) That probably no human power could have relieved our alcoholism; (c) That God could and would if He were sought.

We can start the discussion by asking a volunteer to comment on how he or she came to a basic understanding of what's needed to stay sober.

When and Why We Are
in the Wrong

● ● ●

MODERATOR: AA puts a lot of importance on admitting promptly when we are in the wrong. That's made very explicit in the Tenth Step. We are wise to follow it in our everyday living. But this idea gets a further nudge in *Twelve Steps and Twelve Traditions,* where Bill W. writes: "It is a spiritual axiom that every time we are disturbed, no matter what the cause, there is something wrong *with us.* If somebody hurts us and we are sore, we are in the wrong also."

What is an axiom? One definition is that it's a self-evident truth, something that's so obviously true that no further explanation is required. Well, some explanation is certainly required here, because most of us have assumed that we have a right to be angry if somebody injures us, especially when we don't deserve it. If we go to the parking lot and discover that somebody slammed into our car without leaving a note, don't we have a right to be mad? And if we know who did it, don't we have a right to seek revenge?

The answer, according to Bill W., is always "no." We cannot ever improve ourselves and our position in the world by letting ourselves be disturbed. We should, of course, stand up for our rights, and we should expect people to compensate us for injuries if it is possible to obtain such justice. But we have to avoid the anger and recriminations that often occur during such incidents.

This is not a self-evident truth to many of the people in the world, so that's why we should discuss it. Who will be the first to offer a point of view about this?

When Have We Made a Decision?

• • •

MODERATOR: The Third Step uses the word *decision*—we "made a decision to turn our will and our lives over to the care of God *as we understood Him*." But a question arises in connection with this: What is a decision and when do we know that we've made it?

Decision comes from a Latin word that means "cutting short"—in other words, reducing the choices open to us and eliminating what we think are wrong choices. When we make a firm decision to do something, it usually means dropping any thoughts about alternate plans. But trouble comes when we haven't really made a decision. If we continue to be wishy-washy and go back and forth in deciding whether we really want to quit drinking, we haven't made a decision. We're still hoping that things weren't all that bad in the old life and that maybe we can still drink now and then without suffering the horrible consequences.

We've probably made a real decision when we know with absolute certainty that the old life has to go if we ever hope to have a chance in the new life. When we get to the point of recoiling at the idea of taking a drink, we're probably well into the decision stage. But we're very good at deceiving ourselves, and we also say that alcohol is cunning, baffling, and powerful. When we've made a decision to seek sobriety at all costs, we're also willing to go to any lengths to find it.

Can we help people make such a decision? The best we can do, it seems, is to tell our stories and let nature take its course. Sometimes we have to take quite a beating before we arrive at a real decision.

Who has experience to share about this?

When Have We Taken the Fifth Step?

● ● ●

MODERATOR: Many years ago, a nonalcoholic minister writing in the *AA Grapevine* referred to the Fifth Step as the Big Hump. He compared it to a mountain that had a hump partway up the slope. The hump forced many climbers back, though the climb was actually easy beyond that.

The Fifth Step, he explained, is like that mountain hump. It stops us partway through working the program. False pride and fear make us turn back, because the Fifth Step requires discussing our shortcomings and faults with one other person.

We hear some shallow excuses for taking this Step. One person will say, "I was bankrupt in every department of my life." Another will say, "I think you take that Step when you walk through the door to the AA meeting." Still others will dig in their heels and say that taking the Step isn't even necessary.

The truth is, we don't take the Fifth Step until we've been honest with one other person. Fortunately, only one such person is specified, and it's also agreed that we can parcel portions out to several different people. We are not, however, taking the Step for their benefit. We are looking for our own healing of guilt and shame from the past.

How will we know when we've taken the Step?

❶⓿❶ MEETING STARTERS

There will be a great sense of relief and also an ability to look the world in the eye as never before. It can bring a spiritual release that cannot be found in any other way.

Who will start the discussion about the Fifth Step?

....

....

....

....

....

....

....

....

....

....

....

....

....

When I Feel Better, I'll Do It!

● ● ●

MODERATOR: The topic today is procrastination, and it's best expressed by the statement "When I feel better, I'll do it." This is a very subversive excuse because it suggests that we can't do anything we need to do unless we feel happy and energetic while doing it. The correct statement should be "Do it, and then you'll feel better."

What often happens is that leaving lots of things undone makes us feel bad or worse. Many compulsive people besides alcoholics indulge themselves in their addictions partly as an escape from necessary duties and obligations. Depressed people do this all the time, and it helps compound their depression. It is probably also a problem when people become compulsive about getting certain things done. Most of us have probably met a few such people, and they may make us nervous. But most of us will admit that procrastination is usually more of a problem than compulsive working. We might procrastinate about getting more education or training or put off important things such as paying bills, doing taxes, writing to an old friend, or making repairs.

One solution is to decide to change, just as we also made the decision to stop drinking and to accept the AA program. We don't have to feel better in order to do something; most of the world's work is done by people who aren't necessarily feeling too well all the time.

We can tackle these projects one step at a time. Completing each assignment should give us the courage and confidence to proceed with the next one, and so on. Who knows, we may soon start feeling so good that we won't even have to push ourselves!

I'm sure we can find many examples of this in the group gathered here. Can we have a volunteer to start the discussion?

When Pride Gets in My Way

● ● ●

MODERATOR: When Bill W. wrote *Twelve Steps and Twelve Traditions,* he used the Seven Deadly Sins to discuss taking inventory.

Pride is always listed as the first deadly sin. It can be very deadly for alcoholics because it keeps us from facing or admitting our problems. It also gets in the way of doing anything about these problems.

Here, we're talking about the sick forms of pride. Pride itself is positive when it comes from doing a good job or from one's family. But unhealthy pride holds us in bondage because it defends things we should be releasing.

Unhealthy pride keeps lots of people from admitting that they're alcoholics. Once we've admitted this, it seems silly that we thought it was so hard to do. But a lot of our self-image can be tangled up in our drinking, and we don't like to admit that we're less capable than others in handling our booze.

Pride also gets in the way of making amends, of discussing our defects with another, and in admitting that something we're devoted to is not working. It's possible that many business failures and military blunders are caused by the false pride of the leaders. It takes lots of courage to admit that we are wrong and to face the scorn and criticism that this may involve.

I'd like to throw pride—that is, false or unhealthy pride—out on the table as a topic today. Who will help start the discussion by talking about a time when pride got in the way and what you did to deal with it?

When the Worst Things Become the Best

● ● ●

MODERATOR: We can feel a bit skeptical when people tell us about "blessings in disguise"—the bad breaks that actually turn out well in the long run. Yet that often happens in life, and it's worth discussing at an AA meeting.

A Detroit-area minister who was also an AA member put it this way: "Some of the worst things in my life turned out to be good things. My alcoholism is an example. Becoming an alcoholic is one of the worst things that can happen to a person, but since it led me to AA, it proved to be one of the best things."

That sums it up, and it is also a reason why we shouldn't spend too much time regretting the past. We made a number of choices in past years, and some of them turned out badly. But many of our bad choices also brought us to AA, which we consider to be a great blessing. Therefore, the so-called bad choices weren't so bad after all. This is a good point to remember when we're feeling sorry for ourselves over lost opportunities and the misery of the past. We actually did about as well as we could under the circumstances. If we had known better, we would have done better.

We can be grateful that AA showed us how to

do better. And one of the best ways we can do better is to use the bitter experiences of the past to good advantage by sharing them with others. We are not supposed to regret the past or fear the future. By transforming past mistakes into good lessons, we can see that there is nothing to regret. And by knowing that God is in charge, mistakes we make in the future can also be used to good advantage.

On this subject, there should be a lot to share. Will a volunteer start the discussion?

....

....

....

....

....

....

....

....

....

....

....

Who Is an Alcoholic?

● ● ●

MODERATOR: One of the highest hurdles we face is convincing ourselves that we are alcoholic and need help. It's pretty much agreed that alcoholics can never drink safely again and that most alcoholics need help in finding and maintaining sobriety. This is basic to AA.

But who is an alcoholic? We won't find any one-size-fits-all definition in the AA literature. If we read the Big Book, we'll get an understanding of the alcoholic condition. And there are also two AA pamphlets—*Is AA for Me?* and *Is AA for You?*—that can help people decide whether or not they're alcoholics. Each of these pamphlets points out twelve symptoms of alcoholism—things that are likely to have happened to us if alcoholism is our problem. For example, we couldn't quit drinking, no matter how bad things were becoming. People were calling us drunks. Switching to different drinks did no good. Maybe we had to have a drink the next morning to feel better. We envied people who could control their liquor. We were a problem to other people, and we had problems at home because of our drinking, which was often frantic and compulsive. Yet we denied the problem, even when it caused us to get fired and be rejected by others. We also had blackouts and mounting regrets.

We don't have to have all of these symptoms to be alcoholic. But we're in the danger zone if we have even a few of them.

Many of us have experienced these symptoms. Is a volunteer willing to discuss how these symptoms helped draw him or her into AA?

Whom Can We Fix?

● ● ●

MODERATOR: We've been told that the early AA members in Akron and Cleveland referred to their work as "fixing drunks." That phrase dropped out of use, and for good reason. We know now that we don't fix anybody; people have to fix themselves by accepting and following the program.

But in other ways, some of us try to "fix" people, or at least fix their problems, without realizing that we're doing more than the program calls for. We get people in AA who may have the deep emotional and mental problems the Big Book talks about. Working with such people can be quite a challenge, but many of us try. This effort may come from the goodness of our hearts, but we also may hold the egotistical notion that we somehow have been given the power to fix people. We have no such power.

The nature of the program can push us into situations we'd rather not face. A member can become friendly to a troubled person and then become upset when that person needs help that obviously goes beyond the requirements of the program. She may be a person who can't get to work on time, so her friend buys her an alarm clock. But she forgets to set the clock and still misses work, thus losing her job. So the friend steers her to another opportunity,

178

which she blows just as quickly. Then the friend helps pay the rent or meet some other obligation. It all ends in failure.

This may be a time to get back to the basic idea of carrying the message but not the alcoholic. And yet, when we do take this position, some of us feel guilty about it, as if we are abandoning a friend. And sometimes the troubled friend can also help lay this guilt on us, if we're willing to accept it.

So that brings us to the idea of fixing people. Whom can we fix (or not), and who has had experience with this type of trouble?

....

....

....

....

....

....

....

....

....

....

Why and How We Should Practice Forgiveness

● ● ●

MODERATOR: Here is a tough topic: "why and how we should practice forgiveness." Forgiveness is part of clearing away the wreckage of the past, and the sooner we learn how to do it, the better off we'll be.

The "why" of forgiveness is very simple—it helps us stay sober, and it can enhance our happiness in sobriety.

The "how" of forgiveness is more complicated. What actions can we take that let us forgive? How can we forgive in such a way that we can truly release our resentments and grudges so they don't come back to hurt us? How do we know when we've succeeded in forgiving?

Forgiveness is a three-step process. The first step is to pray sincerely for the offending persons. The second step is to admit our own part in the matter—what we did to help create the situation or make it worse. The third step is to wish the other person well, at least when we think about him or her.

There must be several people here who have thoughts about their own experience with forgiveness. Who will volunteer to share some?

Why Attitude Matters

● ● ●

MODERATOR: In the slang we hear on television, having an "attitude" usually means having a *bad* attitude. But we know in AA that we always have an attitude of one kind or another. Our job is to see that it expresses what we want to think and feel.

We have simple sayings in AA, such as "Change your attitude to gratitude." The truth is that real gratitude does shape attitude in a positive way. Another truth here is that our real attitude can't be concealed. If we're bitter, resentful, jealous, or self-pitying, it shows in our attitude.

There's hardly one of us who doesn't want the *other* person to have a good attitude. We don't like a salesperson who is grumpy, a flight attendant who is snippy, or a waiter who is sullen. What can we do to develop an attitude that will enhance sobriety and smooth relations with others?

1. Attitude reflects the way we think and feel. If we feel kindly toward others, this will bring an attitude of goodwill.
2. Our attitudes will create the kind of atmosphere we live and work in.
3. When working with others in AA, we should remember to work out of a personal need to help ourselves. If we are critical or

condescending toward the suffering alcoholic, that attitude will be a barrier to understanding.

Who will share a personal experience about the benefits of developing a new and better attitude?

....

....

....

....

....

....

....

....

....

....

....

....

Why Did We Drink?

● ● ●

MODERATOR: One of the popular myths of the drinking world and also of general society is that alcoholics have deep and complicated reasons for drinking. We could sometimes use this myth to our own advantage while drinking. For example, a war veteran could draw sympathy and perhaps a few free drinks by giving the impression that the horrors of battle caused him to drink. On a more common level, we could make people think we were drinking because we'd been deserted by a spouse or betrayed by an employer.

Such excuses won't fly in AA, and they are quickly shot down when someone tries to use them. In fact, explaining how we used these excuses to deceive ourselves or others is often a cause for humor.

There is only one reason for drinking that is really true: we drank because we *wanted* to drink. We discovered alcohol to be a marvelous drug that gave us an altered state of mind that seemed better than ordinary reality. Alcohol could take us to distant places. It could transform us into winners. It could help us tell and believe preposterous lies. For a short time, we could be anything we wanted to be.

All of this stopped working in time, of course, and then we had no good choice except finding sobriety in AA. The other choice was to continue drinking and pursuing a course of destruction.

Why did we drink? We drank because we wanted to drink. Who has some thoughts about this to share with the group?

Why Do I Keep Coming Back?

● ● ●

MODERATOR: "Keep coming back" is used in AA as a reminder of the importance of continuance. Whatever we do, we should continue with the program if we expect to continue to receive its benefits. Many people do leave AA—or at least stop going to meetings regularly—without getting drunk. Nonetheless, the people who stick with it and stay with the meetings year after year certainly have an advantage.

But why is it necessary to keep coming back? Shouldn't there be a time when we get loaded up with enough AA to tide us over for the next few years or even a lifetime? After all, it's a simple program, and shouldn't we be able to learn enough in a few years to give us guidance and direction whenever we need it? People who study other subjects don't continue going to school for the rest of their lives, so why should we stay with the meetings?

People outside of AA sometimes criticize us for our strong insistence on the importance of meetings. They have even argued that the meetings are harmful in that the members become dependent on them and feel powerless without them.

So why do we keep coming back? What are our main reasons for coming back after months and years of sobriety? Is it only to protect our sobriety?

Or do we have additional reasons for staying with the meetings?

Who will volunteer some opinions and reasons?

Why Have a Primary Purpose?

• • •

MODERATOR: Most of us don't spend much time reflecting on our primary purpose, but it is important in maintaining sobriety. Our primary purpose, as we state at nearly every meeting, is to maintain our own sobriety and to carry the message to the alcoholic who still suffers.

This applies to the individual as well as to the group and the entire fellowship. Each of us may have a number of purposes competing for our attention, but staying sober ought to be number one if we expect to reach other goals. The program must devote all of its attention to the purpose of helping the individual alcoholic recover.

There will always be people who believe that our success in helping alcoholics gives us the expertise to solve other problems. If we became so involved, however, we would probably weaken our ability to carry out our primary purpose.

This principle of focusing only on our primary purpose has served AA well. Bill W. used the saying, "Shoemaker, stick to thy last." It probably got pretty boring for the old-time shoemakers to do the same job over and over when there were many other interesting jobs to do. But if you're good at one thing, it makes sense to stick to it.

It's also wise for the individual to make continuous sobriety a primary purpose. Who has some thoughts to share about this?

Why Help Is Needed

● ● ●

MODERATOR: People outside the fellowship sometimes question why we place so much stock in the
continued attendance of meetings. It's common to
hear them say, "Do you still go to meetings after all
these years?" Or "Why do you need those people
now that you're sober?" We should not let such
comments bother us or cause us to change our practices. We are the judges of how many meetings we
need and why it might be necessary to attend them
even after years of sobriety.

Some people do get sober without AA's help,
and others stop attending meetings without getting
drunk. That is their affair, and we have no right to
criticize them. Still, we can offer good reasons for
continued attendance at meetings. These have stood
the test of time. One of the main reasons is that
most of us need help in staying sober. Sobriety is an
ongoing process that we establish a day at a time.
We can't stockpile it for future use, because each day
is a new beginning. None of us is immunized from
taking a first drink. AA meetings are our best means
of finding and receiving help. At most meetings,
we'll find people who support us in sobriety and
share their experiences in working the program. We
need them, and they need us.

We must also recognize that the lone individual can be a sitting duck for the pressures and problems that exist in society. The community of AA can be a great help for anybody who feels threatened by the larger world. And if we don't need help at the present moment, we can always benefit by giving it.

May we have a volunteer to discuss how and why we need help?

....

....

....

....

....

....

....

....

....

....

....

....

....

Why Is One Drink So Bad?

● ● ●

MODERATOR: We hear in AA that one drink is too many and a hundred is not enough. This goes along with our belief that the only answer for the alcoholic is to stay away from the first drink at all costs. Others can argue with us about this, but our path is clear: AA sobriety means staying absolutely dry.

We take this so much for granted that we don't ask ourselves why one drink is so bad. All around us, people drink with no problems. The cocktail hour is a time of pleasant conversation and casual drinking with no bad results for most people. In fact, it's called the "happy hour." But if the alcoholic joins in and tries to be one of these casual drinkers, it quickly becomes the "unhappy hour." Why does this have to be?

One thing we can say with certainty is that alcoholics build up patterns of drinking compulsively whenever any amount of alcohol enters the picture. One drink is a signal that it's time to begin with a progression of drinks, and something in the body seems to respond by setting up demands of its own. It's almost as if there is an inner demon that takes over the moment that signal to drink begins. There is also something about one drink that alters one's thinking and pushes out any strong resolutions or inhibitions. As the drink takes hold, a false confidence returns along with a conviction that this time it might be different.

Some believe that people can train themselves to behave responsibly even while drinking. This is called "harm reduction," but most of us know from experience that it doesn't work for us. Drinking clouds our judgment and gives us false ideas of what responsible behavior is. For example, part of the insanity of alcoholism is that the drunk thinks he or she is driving perfectly even while weaving all over the road.

Can we have a volunteer who will offer some thoughts on this subject?

Why Keep Coming Back?

● ● ●

MODERATOR: If you say something kind of "off the wall" at an AA meeting, somebody is likely to say, "Keep coming back." It's said in a kidding way, but "Keep coming back" is important advice. It underscores the importance of continuing on the path that promises real recovery.

Continuance was an idea AA inherited from the Oxford Group. What it conveyed was that we really had to stick to a spiritual program over the long term to get any lasting results from it. It was all too easy to get an initial burst of enthusiasm that carried us along and then lose it all by sitting back and forgetting the things that helped us get well.

We see the same thing happen in AA. We come into the program and are greatly relieved and delighted to find an answer. Many things start to go better in our lives. We might get our bosses off our backs or convince a judge to give us a break. It's also nice to wake up without a hangover and to remember what we did the night before. Life gets better quickly.

But then boredom sets in, and we reach a stage of diminishing returns. We hear people saying the same thing over and over again at meetings. Now that we have sobriety, there doesn't seem to be all that much benefit in continuing to return.

When this happens, we're in real danger because alcohol is always there to welcome us back. The meetings may seem boring at times, but they do work in helping us stay continuously sober. Most of us feel we need them.

So "Keep coming back" is great advice. Who will pick this up and offer some additional thoughts about it?

Why Resentment Leads the Pack

● ● ●

MODERATOR: Alcoholics usually have several problems that go along with drinking or are aggravated
by it. But the Big Book tells us that resentment is the
number one offender. "It destroys more alcoholics
than anything else," Bill W. wrote. "From it stem all
forms of spiritual disease, for we have been not only
mentally and physically ill, we have been spiritually
sick." Resentment does get a lot of attention, and
most AA members are surprisingly honest about it.
But maybe we should ask why it seems to be the
number one offender, the one thing we should
guard against almost as carefully as we guard against
the first drink.

The best way to understand the danger of resentment is to recall the times it sideswiped us while
we were still drinking. We could be having a great
day, and then something could happen that would
release a flood of resentment. Before we knew it, we
were drunk. It happened that way many times for
most of us.

One tricky part of these resentments is that
most of the time, we thought they were justified. If
somebody stiffed us in some way, we thought we
had a right to be angry. Sometimes we even felt that
we had the moral high ground in feeling indigna-
tion or rage.

But we need to learn that nothing is justified if it leads us into taking a drink or plunges us into a terrible mood. So it's necessary to keep this resentment in check if we expect to succeed in staying sober.

How does the group feel about this? Do we have a volunteer to start the discussion?

Why Should We Make Amends?

● ● ●

MODERATOR: Our topic today is on making amends. More to the point, it is on why we should make amends.

Two of our Steps deal with making amends. Step Eight calls for making a list of all the people we've harmed and being willing to make amends to them. Step Nine is actually making the amends: "Made direct amends to such people wherever possible, except when to do so would injure them or others."

Why is it necessary to do this? The reason is simple: it's part of getting sober and maintaining sobriety. It's also part of straightening out twisted relations from the past. We can agree that hanging on to this wreckage of the past is harmful when we're trying to live on a new basis.

We have a great example of amends making in Dr. Bob's story. Bill W. had brought him the message and given him hope, but after a few weeks, Dr. Bob took a trip that turned into an awful bender. Waking up from this nightmare, he told Bill he was going to do whatever it took to get sober and stay that way. He was a proud man who was fearful of being barred from his profession. But he took the plunge that very day and went around to visit certain people and to tell them what he was trying to do. He came home a happy man and never took another drink for the rest of his life.

It doesn't always work out according to our expectations. There's a risk in making amends. It may require swallowing some pride and making amends to people who have harmed us in return. This does not really matter in the long run, because our purpose is to deal with our own part of whatever trouble occurred. We must focus on our part of the issue and clean that up, and we have then made amends.

Now let's hear from a few people about their experiences in making amends. It will help us to know why you made amends, perhaps how you went about it, and whether it made a difference in your life.

Why Suffer to Get Well?

● ● ●

MODERATOR: The second edition of the Big Book featured a story titled "The Professor and the Paradox," which introduced four paradoxes in connection with AA and recovery. The author defined a paradox as a statement that appears to be false but that, upon examination, can be true in certain instances. One of these four paradoxes is "We suffer to get well."

Because suffering and sickness go together, this does seem to be a contradiction. But maybe we have to understand that our sickness is alcoholism, and we were medicating ourselves for the emotional pain that we felt even before we became alcoholic in the first place. Alcohol betrayed us, however, and eventually caused more suffering than the emotional pain we were trying to escape. It also took immense suffering to convince us that we needed the AA program.

It is not easy to admit that one needs the kind of help that AA offers. Some of us felt shame that we ever had to seek AA's help in the first place. So it was only a great deal of suffering that convinced us we needed to make the move.

Once we get sober, our suffering does not end. There are many times in sobriety when we would like to escape from the boredom and self-doubt that plague us. Going through these periods can bring about suffering, but we have to endure these times if we hope to live. "No pain, no gain" could be the guide for these periods.

Once we're fairly well, the suffering decreases. But suffering is part of the human condition, and we cannot always avoid it. We can at least be grateful that we no longer cause our own suffering or cause others to suffer.

Who will offer experience about suffering to get well?

Why Work the Tenth Step?

● ● ●

MODERATOR: Step Ten suggests we continue to do something that most human beings find difficult—admitting when we're wrong. Yet this can benefit us no matter how we apply it. When we were drinking, we were doing something that was destructive to our future and was also harming others. Until we admitted this, there was no way this sorry life could change.

Even in sobriety—in fact, especially in sobriety—we can find problems growing out of our personal shortcomings. If we root these out and do something about them, the door is open for constructive change. If we improve our attitude on the job, for example, we improve our chances for advancement. Our personal relationships can improve when we work on selfishness and other character defects.

It may seem that we are admitting complete failure when we take the Tenth Step. But we are really only recognizing temporary problems and correcting them so that our lives will be better and happier.

Now I'd like to open this topic up for discussion around the table. I hope someone will offer an example of how working the Tenth Step may have required a short-term struggle but turned out to produce long-term benefits.

Willingness Is the Key

● ● ●

MODERATOR: When we hear about people who slip, we might also hear that they weren't willing to do what's needed to stay sober. Perhaps they weren't honest with themselves. Perhaps they didn't go to enough meetings. Perhaps they were spending too much time thinking about the old life.

Whatever the reasons, it usually comes back to willingness. We're told again and again that willingness is the key to sobriety. If we really want to stay sober, AA can help us. But we have to be willing to let the program work for us—and to work the program. I believe we can find an effective topic for this meeting in willingness. Maybe we can hear from somebody who had to work through this problem in order to get sober and stay that way. Or maybe some are wondering if they have enough willingness to succeed in the program.

To start the discussion, could somebody offer a clear-cut example of the way true willingness brought about desired results? All of us have known people in the program who had repeated slips and then suddenly got their act together and found continuous sobriety. What was it that brought this about? And can people really develop willingness just by deciding it's a good thing and going for it?

Will somebody at the table comment on this subject?

....

....

....

....

....

....

....

....

....

....

....

....

....

....

....

Winning the Boredom Battle

● ● ●

MODERATOR: We talk about some heavy problems in AA but hardly ever mention such a simple subject as boredom. When did anybody ever say that he or she had a slip just because of continuing boredom? Do we ever look at boredom and ask how we can deal with it constructively so we're not led to places where we shouldn't go?

One answer for boredom is excitement. That's not a very good answer, however, because it's not healthy to seek continuously the kind of stimulation that excitement gives. We sometimes looked for exciting experiences in bars, though we didn't find them very often. But even *seeking* excitement is a form of excitement, so that became part of our problem. Another answer for boredom is simply to accept it as part of the human experience. That is not a very attractive answer, and it seems like a form of resignation—resigning ourselves to be bored and unhappy much of the time. Yet if there is no alternative except drinking, it's okay to accept boredom with the knowledge that "this too will pass someday." A large number of AA members have successfully dealt with boredom in this way and imply as much in their talks.

People who are interested in their work and hobbies have suitable answers to boredom. The only risk in this is becoming a workaholic or using the hobby to replace AA activity. Finally, there's a lot to be said for the answers that AA itself gives for boredom. Perhaps it wasn't planned that way, but an AA meeting will help a person get through a lonely evening. A person on a business trip to a strange town can always count on an AA meeting to fill up an evening. AA also has other boredom-fighting ideas. In any case, boredom is something we have to deal with, one way or another. Who would like to discuss it?

OTHER TITLES THAT MAY INTEREST YOU:

Walk in Dry Places
Mel B.

For each day of the year, *Walk in Dry Places* offers a meditation and a prayer. The author's reflective, insightful explorations of the deeper issues of recovery speak to those new to recovery, as well as to those who have achieved long-term sobriety. Softcover, 400 pp.
Order No. 1468

Twenty-Four Hours a Day

Featuring an inspirational thought, meditation, and prayer for each day of the year, *Twenty-Four Hours a Day* offers encouragement, support, and wisdom to help you continue down the path of spiritual and personal growth. Softcover, 400 pp.
Order No. 5093

The Little Red Book

This classic is one of the most-used and best-loved study companions to the Big Book, *Alcoholics Anonymous*. It offers those new to recovery—and those seeking a deeper meaning in the Twelve Steps—advice on program work, sponsorship, spirituality, and much more. Softcover, 160 pp.
Order No. 1034

Hazelden books are available at fine bookstores everywhere. To order directly from Hazelden, call 1-800-328-9000 or visit www.hazelden.org/bookstore.